SERIES EDITOR: MARION BOULTON STROUD

DESIGN: TAKAAKI MATSUMOTO

INTRODUCTION BY HAROLD KODA

WRITTEN BY AMY WILKINS

ACADIA SUMMER ARTS PROGRAM

Published by Acadia Summer Arts Program

Marion Bolton Stroud, Publisher and Series Editor

Takaaki Matsumoto, Matsumoto Incorporated, New York,
Producer and Designer

Amy S. Wilkins, Matsumoto Incorporated, New York,
Manager of Publications

Pamela T. Barr, Editor

Printed and bound by Nissha Printing Co., Ltd., Kyoto, Japan

Copyright © 2010 by Acadia Summer Arts Program

All text © 2010 Matsumoto Incorporated, New York
All photography © Matsumoto Incorporated, New York

Photography Credits:
Will Brown: 77 top, 81; Courtesy The Fabric Workshop and
Museum: 88 bottom, 89, 159 bottom; Courtesy Sazaby,
Inc.: 52–53; Keld Helmer-Petersen: 147; Wataru Kumano: 6;
Takaaki Matsumoto: 69, 100 top, 107 bottom, 144, 163, 170
bottom; Robert Pettus, Courtesy the Pulitzer Foundation
for the Arts: 114; Takashi Sekiguchi: 46; Mikio Sekita: 7–10,
15, 17, 23, 25, 39, 44–45, 47–48, 58–61, 62–63, 65 top and
bottom, 67–68, 70–73, 75–76, 79, 82 top, 83, 88 top, 96, 97
top, 98–99, 105–6, 108–9, 115, 118, 120–22, 129, 136–39,
141–43, 145–46, 152, 154, 156–58, 159 top, 160 top, 161–62,
165–69, 171–79; Hiroshi Sugimoto: 97 bottom, 107 middle;
Matt Wargo: 65 middle.

Library of Congress Control Number: 2010901839
ISBN: 978-0-9797642-3-3

Available through D.A.P./Distributed Art Publishers
155 Sixth Avenue, 2nd Floor
New York, New York 10013
Tel: (212) 627.1999
Fax: (212) 627.9484
www.artbook.com

I had the very good fortune to meet Takaaki Matsumoto in spring 1995, when he was designing a catalogue for the exhibition "Material Dreams" at the Gallery at Takashimaya. The Fabric Workshop and Museum assembled an artwork by Jim Hodges for the exhibition—a large curtain of silk flowers that had been invisibly sewn together. When I met Takaaki and saw the catalogue, I knew immediately that he was a designer of exceptional talent, sensitivity, and humor and a true genius of his time. The catalogue was intimate and poetic and perfectly communicated the spirit of the artwork. He also made work seem like fun, with his infectious laughter and his serious and deep design philosophy.

I immediately invited him and his wife, Julie Losch, also a designer, to Maine to be my houseguests, and Takaaki shyly suggested some design ideas he had for the Acadia Summer Arts Program. From there, the floodgates of design opened. It was as if we had asked him for a cup of water and it turned out that we got an ever-flowing river of design ideas. Since then, there is scarcely anything that he has not designed for us: publications, websites, A.S.A.P. stationery that changes colors every year, the FWM identity, T-shirts, caps, bags, guest books for A.S.A.P. guests and staff, postcards, and invitations. He likes to say, "Give me the material and I'll start to think about it," and then by the end of the day or sooner he'll have come back with a brilliant idea.

Takaaki created the most brilliant design for the book *New Material as New Media*, published by MIT Press, which won the "Franny" prize at the 2003 American Association of Museums Publication Competition. The following year he designed *Goddess: The Classical Mode* for the Costume Institute at the Metropolitan Museum of Art. Harold Koda, the chief curator, called him and said, "Have you ever won this award before? We've just won the "Franny" prize for *Goddess*." To which Takaaki had to admit, modestly, "Yes, I won it last year for *New Material as New Media* with the Fabric Workshop and Museum." His humility is everlasting, and everyone who has used him as their designer has been rewarded beyond belief, both with his genius and his wonderful character. Ellsworth Kelly, for whom Takaaki has designed many beatiful catalogues, remarked, "Takaaki is the only designer that does not try to mimic my artwork."

Takaaki understands far better than I do what A.S.A.P. wants to be, what the artists' works want to be, and tells the story that we can't even begin to articulate without his help. His favorite phrase is "I've got an idea," and his most recent one is our new A.S.A.P. book series, the idea being that we will publish books that focus on individual artists, curators, architects, and others—we have already published volumes on William Wegman and Marcia Tucker—who have been guests at the program.

In the many projects that we have worked on together, fully realized designs seem to spring from the smallest description of an idea. Although attempting to describe how or why the designs succeed is beyond my abilities, I can say that there is always a combination of intuition and indescribable logic to his creations. As Ann Temkin, the chief curator of painting and sculpture of the Museum of Modern Art, described working with Takaaki, "He grasped the nuances and idiosyncrasies of the argu-ment behind the exhibition, and . . . [devised] deceptively and marvel-ously simple solutions for complicated problems." That is the essence of a Matsumoto design: a presentation of complex, nuanced subject matter that is at once elegant and comprehensible.

Early twentieth-century shop sign for
Matsumoto Paper, Kanazawa, Japan
Opposite: late nineteenth-century
hangi (wood printing die) used at the
Matsumoto paper shop

Born in Kanazawa, Japan, Takaaki Matsumoto was expected to assume his father's title and responsibilities at Matsumoto Paper, the family papermaking business. The Matsumotos adopted their trade in the mid-nineteenth century, during the early Meiji era, the period of Japan's aggressive social reorganization and modernization, when laws were enacted to pacify the clan-based military class. Kanazawa was once the seat of the powerful Maeda samurai clan and rivaled Kyoto and Edo (present-day Tokyo) as a cultural force. In Japan members of the privileged classes, including the professional warrior, embraced a philosophy that blurred the lines between martial rigor and refined cultural pursuits. Kanazawa's samurai culture emphasized the rituals and practices of the aesthete, such as *chanoyu* (the tea ceremony), *ikebana* (flower arranging), calligraphy, and poetry as much as swordsmanship or the other martial arts. Matsumoto Paper may be seen, then, as the successful merging of the sophisticated cultivation and rigorous ethos of the samurai with the aesthetics at the core of the artisanal refinements of Japanese papermaking.

Spared the devastation of firebombing in World War II, Kanazawa retains much of the character of prewar Japan in its carefully maintained architecture, extensive historic districts, and renowned gardens from the past. Thus, raised in a family with an artisanal enterprise located in one of Japan's renowned cultural communities, Matsumoto would not dispute the impact of his early experiences and his fascination with the details of

Knoll International catalogue, 1985

Three Women: Madeleine Vionnet, Claire McCardell, and Rei Kawakubo, Fashion Institute of Technology, 1987

Rebecca Horn, Solomon R. Guggenheim Museum, 1993

traditional Japanese culture. His life has, however, been characterized by a distancing of himself physically, if not psychically, from his roots.

His is a course that perhaps began with his parents' decision to send him to Jiyu Gakuen, a progressive preparatory academy in Tokyo. (Frank Lloyd Wright designed the original building.) In an environment that prized independence and self-sufficiency—for example, first-year students were directed to construct desks, chairs, and bookshelves for their own use in the dormitory—Matsumoto began his break from the expectations of his family. While still a student, he was exposed to the exciting conceptual and narrative possibilities of graphic design at an exhibition that included the work of Ikko Tanaka and Shigeo Fukuda, among others. The impact of the exhibition persists for him, and Matsumoto still cites his strong affinity for the work of Tanaka, characterized by its transfiguration of a definitive Japanese aesthetic into an international design sensibility.

When he graduated from Jiyu Gakuen, Matsumoto intended to prepare for a career in the arts with continued studies in Tokyo but was encouraged by a family friend in the design field to pursue his interests abroad. Moving to California, he was admitted into an accelerated program in Graphic and Packaging Design at the Art Center College of Design in Pasadena and, while there, had the opportunity to attend the groundbreaking "Japan at Aspen" International Design Conference of 1979. As a guide and translator for the eminent participants from the Japanese avant-garde, including Issey Miyake, Tadanori Yokoo, Toshi Katayama, Nagai Kazumasa, Kisho Kurokawa, and Tanaka, among others, Matsumoto was exposed to the most innovative Japanese design and witnessed the international reach of its influential cross-cultural aesthetic.

Although he was encouraged by his success in California and was offered a position at a prestigious firm in Chicago, Matsumoto chose instead to investigate the possibilities of a career in New York. His first job, at Gips and Balkind in Manhattan, introduced him, through Phil Gips, his mentor at the firm, to a design approach that prized novel typography and an eclectic, sometimes historicist-inflected contemporaneity. If Gips underscored a design approach with a post-1960s creative exuberance, Matsumoto's move to Knoll International in 1982 focused his vision on the strict principles of high modernism. But even there, the impact of a rigorous International Style was tempered, particularly in the final years of his tenure, by industrial minimalist and post-modernist collaborations, notably with Robert Venturi, that had begun to percolate through the firm.

By the time he partnered with Michael McGinn to co-found the independent design firm M Plus M Incorporated, which then evolved into Matsumoto Incorporated, Matsumoto had created a body of work predicated on modernist principles but with the essential programmatic and communicative functions of his designs always cloaked in an accumulation of legible and precise aesthetic decisions. While at Knoll, he had juggled a number of outside projects for the American Craft Museum, National Geographic, and *Art in America* magazine. These private endeavors, with a client base of art professionals and cultural institutions, came to represent some of Matsumoto's most successful collaborations.

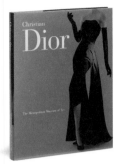

Christian Dior, The Metropolitan Museum of Art, 1996

Indeed, while Matsumoto addresses every project with an analysis of its program and a clarification of its essential goals—what it needs to accomplish and communicate—he has stated that each one actually begins with his affinity for, or interest in, the client. When asked how he would describe his work, Matsumoto says, "I'm involved in communication: with the client, or the subject of a project, such as an artist who is the focus of a monograph, or the intentions of a client, or the reason for a product. It is all about communication, in both the process and the result." That so many of his collaborations have been with the greatest artists of our time suggests his ability to penetrate and interpret the intentions of the critical eye and creative mind. His philosophy was articulated in a conversation he had with Richard Koshalek, the director of the Hirshhorn Museum and former president of the Art Center College of Design, when he stated simply, "The goal is always to let the message come through clearly, and the design should support that message but not overshadow it." This apparent self-effacement is reflected in the subtle strategies of his designs, his elegant lucidity invariably resulting in resolutions of pronounced elegance.

Sugimoto: Portraits, Solomon R. Guggenheim Museum, 1999

Matsumoto has suggested that he combines something of the formalism of the Bauhaus with a concept-oriented approach. He is both and neither: his designs frequently evoke a Swiss classicism, but they avoid the rigidity of modernist ideology; his work is often imbued with a witty conceptual twist, but the humor is more likely to elicit a smile than a laugh. The trajectory of Takaaki Matsumoto's personal and professional life suggests the heterogeneous nature of his aesthetic, one informed by explicitly Japanese concepts but expressed through the clarified language of Western modernism. For example, his fluency in the international design vocabulary is informed by a particularly Japanese concept of *shibui*, extraordinary refinement in the guise of apparent simplicity. In his graphic and product designs, Matsumoto's signature is not the stridency of the bold stroke but rather the harmony of the impeccably considered detail and of the quiet but assertive beauty of materials both extraordinary and prosaic that mediate the reductive and the decorative, the elemental and the refined.

Luc Tuymans, San Francisco Museum of Modern Art and Wexner Center for the Arts, 2009

As much as type and image, the materials employed by Matsumoto, whether artisanal or industrial, convey and underscore the conceptual underpinnings of his designs. He has described how as a child he loved to play among the vertiginous stacks of paper stored on the second floor of his family house. It is an image that provides a visual metaphor for his literal and figurative immersion in the traditional arts, an exposure further enhanced by the broader context of growing up in Kanazawa, where artisanal traditions are maintained to this day. If his exposure to the refined aesthetics and expressive materiality of traditional Japanese papers is still manifest in his work, it may be seen in many of his projects that are specifically predicated on the surface, weight, and density of paper or on the clear relief of a letterpress imprint. Given the terse gestures of his style, Matsumoto's choice of materials takes on significant aesthetic weight. Often surprisingly industrial, they are, however, always selected in faintly muted variations: corrugated plastic is given a translucent vinyl skin, aluminum sheeting a matte rather than polished finish, or black granite a dulled, almost porous surface. The effect is at once powerful and veiled. Although he is an admirer of the work of Joseph Beuys and Alexander Rodchenko, he is rarely seduced in his own work by the coarse Arte Povera–like emotionalism of the former or the slick machine-age utopianism of the latter. Instead, Matsumoto is a modernist with a poetic core that appears to preclude the extreme resolutions of even his favorite artists.

Square (detail of installation), 1989.
The Edward C. Blum Design Laboratory
at Fashion Institute of Technology,
New York

In fact, when asked which fine artists have inspired him, Matsumoto has also cited Marcel Duchamp and Felix Gonzalez-Torres. Here, his conceptual affinities seem to be more closely aligned, for much of Matsumoto's graphic work requires the active manipulation of his pieces for a full understanding of his concept, a quiet form of Dadaist play. Closed or folded, his designs seem complete and readily apprehended, but this first comprehension is invariably partial. Only in the opening and unfolding of his work does one confront the fuller intentions of the piece. This transformative possibility extends to Matsumoto's product designs. The jagged Art Moderne hands of a watch become at noon the silhouette of the Empire State Building. On another, the markings of the watch face have been displaced to the crystal. The discrete units of time are enhanced by their own shifting shadows on the watch's blank face.

A 1983 exhibition at the Edward C. Blum Design Laboratory at the Fashion Institute of Technology in New York revealed a more expressionistic facet of his work, with an idiosyncratic palette and a barely suppressed post-modern agitation in its forms. He has said that the bolder graphic language displayed on the walls of the gallery and in a series of posters created for the installation represented his more personal taste, unfiltered by collaboration. It is a sensibility aligned to the work of the Tokyo designers who emerged in the mid-1970s, the participants at Aspen, but informed by Matsumoto's strict impulse to order. In the posters, textural brushwork frames a grid-based pattern. The patternmaking has been subjected to a series of rigorously restrained and restraining criteria. Squares, in descending dimensions by half, are rotated in mathematical sequences. Matsumoto's inherent conceptual rigor results in a counterintuitive visual *koan*: severely limited organizing principles and a strict orthogonal geometry yield an astonishing array of fractal-like variations. Against a field of undifferentiated chaos, it is order that emerges in infinite multiplicity.

Matsumoto's work, as an artistic enterprise, is the result of a combination of intellect, strategic methodology, technical facility, and aesthetic innovation. His experience, with its roots in the most conservative cultural traditions of Japan, forged under the disparate influences of the Art Center, an internationalist Japanese avant-garde, Phil Gips as the personification of the New York School, and the pure modernism of Knoll, has evolved into a unified signature—a style at once readily identifiable but communicated through the most elusive qualities of economy, material perfection, and conceptual clarity. Ultimately, the power of his designs resides in the elegance of his strategy to convey ideas. Beautiful artifacts of paper, metal, stone, wood, and cloth are sensual but reductive manifestations of Matsumoto's self-described role as a facilitator of communication. In the visual cacophony that surrounds us, his work establishes the compelling power of the meaningful, content-rich whisper.

● Art Center College of Design

Since its founding in 1930, the Art Center College of Design has incorporated an orange dot in its logo. It is a matter of dispute how the dot originated or whose idea it was, but it persisted and attempts to do away with it were met with protest by both students and faculty. When the college decided to update its visual identity for its seventy-fifth anniversary, in 2005, the dot was retained but the typography was redesigned. A strong but flexible identity system was essential for the Art Center to communicate its commitment to creativity and innovation. The idea that emerged was a "white box," a graphic template that would be recognizable as the Art Center but would allow the college's different departments to implement it as they saw fit. The final logo design combines the orange dot with the school's full name, set in Univers. Rules for implementing the logo were specific—colors were limited to the orange and gray selected for the primary logo, plus all black or all white for certain applications—but its simplicity also allowed diverse methods of application. As long as the logo was applied consistently there was freedom to design materials creatively.

The stationery was made with a custom watermark of randomly scattered dots that are visible when the sheet of paper is held up to the light. Folders, printed in solid red, magenta, and orange, were embossed with dots of various sizes. Simplicity coupled with flexibility gave rise to many different incarnations of the Art Center's identity in its visual communication materials.

● Art Center College of Design

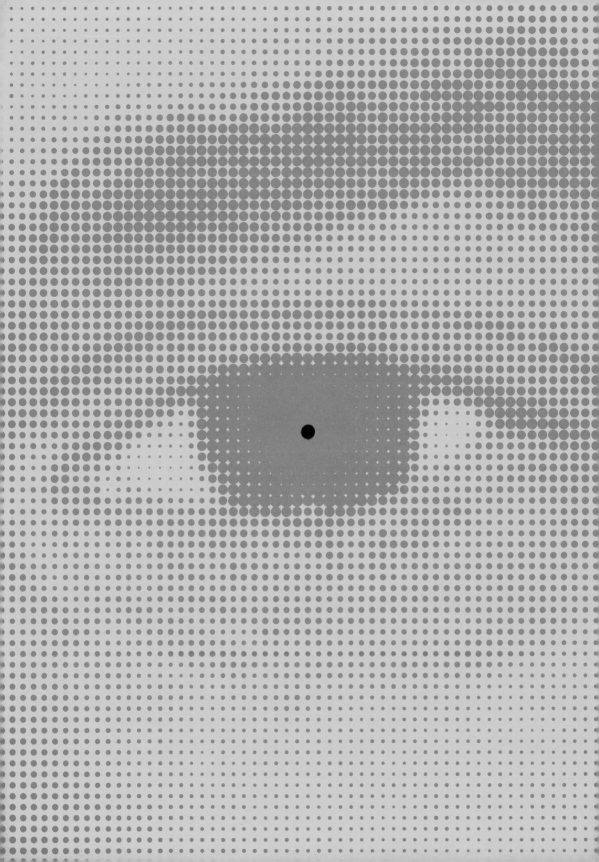

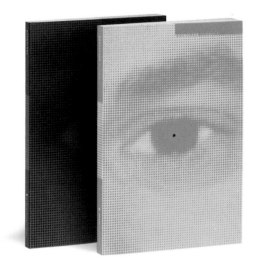

Boundless is a two-volume collection of interviews with prominent Art Center alumni. Each volume contains twenty interviews with an accompanying photograph of the subject. The budget allowed for only two-color offset printing, so the design had to be visually interesting without containing color photography. In addition to this constraint, the photographs of the alumni were low resolution, which turned into an advantage: they were enlarged drastically so that the images broke into dots to create an effect similar to Pointillism. Each was cropped to show only the eyes and the nose of the subject, and these were used as the divider pages for each interview. They were all positioned so that the irises of the eyes aligned. The full portrait was reproduced at a very small scale, a half-inch square, at the bottom center of the right-hand page.

After the book was bound, a one-eighth-inch hole, the diameter of the dot in the Art Center's logo, was drilled through it, piercing each eye in the center. This was an inexpensive way to add an element of surprise and whimsy to the book.

The size and the leading of the type were determined based on the diameter of the hole. There also had to be an area of sufficient space around the hole so that none of the type would be cut off when the pages were finally bound and trimmed. There is always a margin of error, or tolerance (typically one-sixteenth of an inch), for how much a sheet will move up or down, left or right, when it is trimmed. To clear the tolerance, the centerline of each page had to be hand-kerned around the hole.

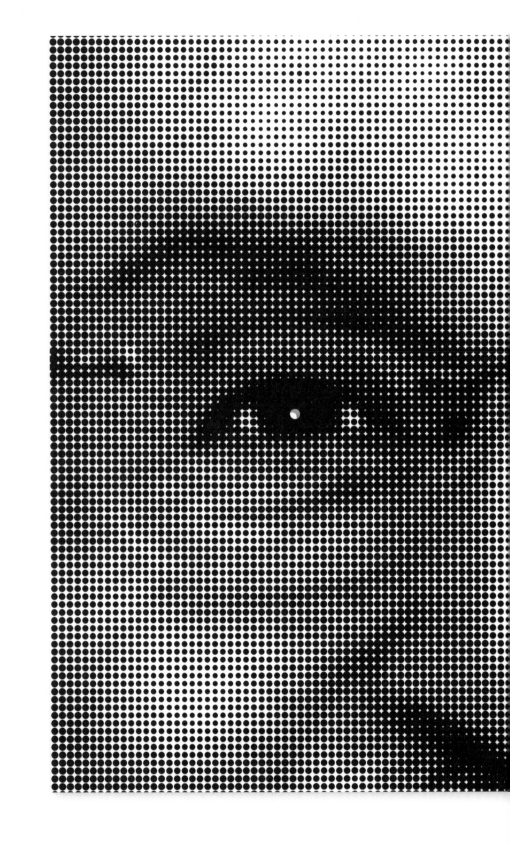

RAFAEL DAVIDSON

PRODUCT DESIGN '62

Rafael Davidson was born in the Canary Islands, Spain, and moved to Mexico toward the end of World War II. After attending Art Center he worked on the design of General Motors' exhibit for the 1964/65 New York World's Fair, and on Ford's Mustang project. In 1967 he returned to Mexico as head of Zeerhut/Veeder/Shimano Design, the first industrial design office in the country. Later he opened Davidson and Associates, was design director of Landor Associates, and vice president of Young and Rubicam in charge of its subsidiary CYB (Cato/Yasamura/Behaegel) in Mexico and San Francisco. While in Mexico he won more than a dozen design prizes and awards. He also designed the renowned line of "Mexico Exporta" postal stamps.

From 1987 to 1998 he lived and cruised on a 30-foot sailboat and taught during the summers at Art Center and the Academy of Art College in San Francisco. In 1999 Davidson returned to Mexico and was given a Life Achievement Award by Quorum (Design Council of Mexico). He is now a teacher and advisor for the Industrial Design department of the Instituto Tecnológico de Monterrey, Mexico City campus.

Art Center: *What do you see as a designer's responsibility?*

Rafael Davidson: The first cliché that comes to mind is social responsibility, but I don't really believe that. I think that social responsibility is often misinterpreted as the right (or even the moral obligation) to push your own beliefs and values onto others "for their own good." I much prefer the Zen Buddhist attitude of being yourself and getting involved and connected with others, with respect and a spirit of compassion. I believe that a designer, most of all, should be creative and true to himself or herself. In other words, a designer should design.

AC: *You're talking about having integrity in who you are and being responsible for what you put into the world.*

RD: I think so, and I think that starts from within: your concepts, your sensitivity and your feelings of connectedness and respect.

AC: *Are there aspects of your Art Center education that have stayed with you?*

RD: Oh, yes, Art Center changed my life completely. I was studying mechanical engineering in Mexico and having a really hard time with it. So I thought, I'm going to go to the United States; maybe they can teach it better there. I came to this country and went to Antioch College. But I still had troubles with engineering, and then I realized it was me, and not the schools. Let me tell you, my self-esteem hit bottom! My art teacher suggested that I go into industrial design instead, although I had   never heard of it before. So I applied to Art Center and they said: "You need to send a portfolio." "A what?" Well, the little samples that I sent were laughable, but they accepted me on a probationary basis. I had two semesters to prove myself. In spite of the pressure, Art Center was, for me, total release, total freedom, right from the start. I loved it when I would put my work up on the wall and the teacher liked it and the other students would say, "Whoa, that's wild!" At the end of the two semesters my probation was lifted and General Motors gave me a scholarship. It did wonders for my self-esteem.

AC: *Many people say that what they got from Art Center was the exact opposite.*

RD: My father was German, very rigid and conservative. He liked it when I was studying engineering. He wanted me to "be realistic," "practical," to "play it safe" and not do "crazy things." That was the voice I heard growing up. But Art Center gave me permission to do whatever I wanted. It gave me freedom to be creative and be myself. On top of that, it gave me the tools and skills to express myself and make a living. I couldn't have asked for more. I will be forever thankful.

AC: *It sounds like there's a big connection between creativity and freedom for you.*

RD: Absolutely. Something else that had a strong influence on me was the Whole Earth Catalogue. It showed how you could design your own life, and where to get the tools you

Viewbook, Art Center College of

Design, 2008

The main printed recruitment tool for the college is its biannual catalogue, and the 2007–8 edition was the first to present the Art Center's new visual identity. Creating a cover was difficult because the college has departments for fine art, filmmaking, transportation design, and other disciplines, so one image cannot adequately represent all its facets. A simple white cover with die-cut holes randomly scattered across the front was the solution. The only printing is the orange and gray logo. When the cover is closed, the holes display various colors but the overall effect is quiet and subtle. Opening the cover reveals a page full of brightly colored circles floating like bubbles. (The graphic element of the bubbles was also used for the *Viewbook*, a smaller recruitment booklet sent to potential students before they receive the large admissions catalogue.) Although some of the colored circles overlap, the die-cut holes, which are the same size as the dot in the logo, were placed so that only one color shows through each hole; the hole never reveals two colors or a white spot.

The mailing container presented another opportunity to play with the dot theme. Fabricated from clear bubble wrap, the mailer has hundreds of circles floating in a tight, regular pattern on the outside of the catalogue. The recipient can see the catalogue through the envelope, so the two layers of dots reinforce the visual identity. The mailer also had the virtue of being simple to produce; the bubble-wrap envelopes were made to the specifications of the catalogue and did not need to be printed.

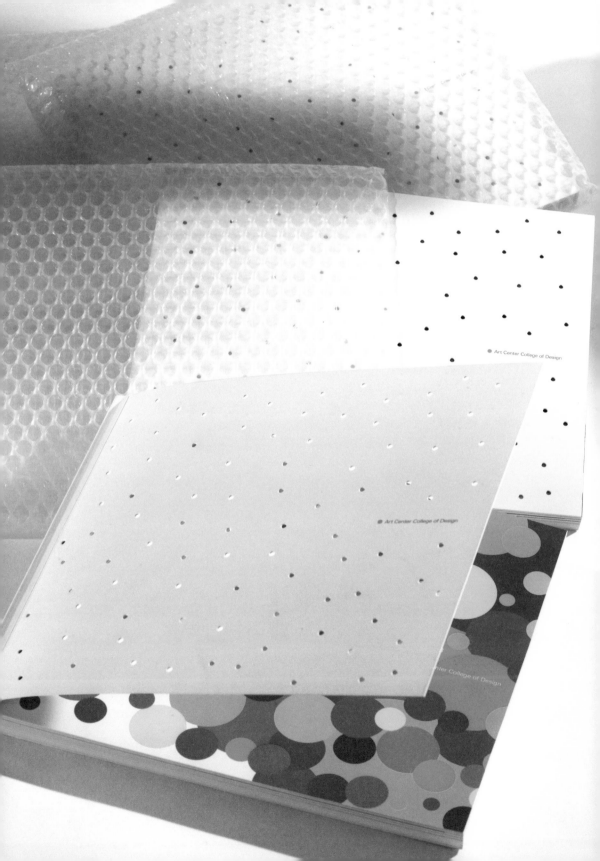

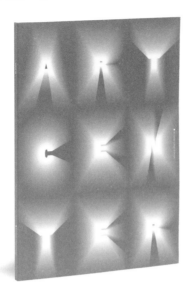

For this recruitment catalogue, the concept was to project a friendly, open image to prospective students. The first decision was to make the catalogue oversized, similar to a tabloid magazine. At more than fourteen inches high, it is much larger than most other college recruitment catalogues. The large size was feasible only because the nuts-and-bolts information about admission requirements, course listings, and faculty biographies, which had always been included in previous catalogues and accounted for half of their pages, was eliminated and placed on the college's website. A smaller page count made it possible to enlarge the dimensions of the book without increasing the budget. Large type, generously sized reproductions of the students' work (the main interest of prospective students), and plenty of white space create a breezy feel. To enhance the catalogue's approachability, portraits of the students and faculty are used throughout. Each department chair chose eight students to represent the department's portfolio, and each student was given a page in the catalogue to display his or her work. Along with the student's work, each portfolio page contains a silhouetted, full-length portrait of the student and a quotation describing some aspect of the Art Center experience. The portraits and testimonials give the book a personal quality and become a design element throughout.

The Student Gallery is a showcase of exceptional student work that helps define the Art Center experience. Carefully selected by Department Chairs each term, the work on display reflects the incredible range of talent across the various disciplines.

Art Center students come from diverse backgrounds and bring their unique, personal experiences to the College.

"Student organizations at Art Center are an excellent resource for social and professional networking among peers and provide an engaging atmosphere where students can decompress."
—Tim Anderson, Entertainment Design, fifth term
Pictured above is the student-run EcoCouncil, which works closely with Art Center faculty and administration to find practical and creative solutions to reduce Art Center's ecological impact.

"Art Center seems to be the only design college that is truly international. With people coming from all over the world, this cultural mix stimulates creativity and ultimately prepares you to take a job anywhere in the world." —Henrik Fisker, Transportation Design, '89

Why Art Center?

One of the world's preeminent art and design colleges, Art Center College of Design is renowned for its culture of innovation, rigorous transdisciplinary curriculum and extensive relationships with industry. For almost 80 years, Art Center has played a crucial role in the professional development of a distinguished community of artists and designers who have created globally recognized work and served as leaders in major design, business, civic and cultural organizations around the world.

Even more, Art Center stands out among other art and design colleges for its deep level of engagement in critical issues affecting society on a larger scale. Many of the College's programs and projects focus on contemporary, real-world challenges, granting students extraordinary opportunities to immerse themselves in complex design problems. The innovative solutions that students develop are a testament to the power of design to inspire positive social change.

Most of today's leading businesses acknowledge that in the competitive global market, innovation is the great differentiator. In that light, Art Center's alumni are pursued by some of the world's most influential organizations. These companies know that our students not only produce superb portfolios, but also have experience in collaborative, real-world settings. Partnerships with major corporations and organizations begin in the classroom and studio, and continue through internships, mentorships, fellowships, lectures, presentations and recruitment events. More than 90 percent of Art Center students find employment in their chosen fields within their first year after graduation. Many others are inspired to create their own entrepreneurial businesses and studios.

Art Center College of Design was named by Business Week as one of the Top Innovation & Design Schools in both 2006 and 2007.

Art Center's state-of-the-art facilities and technology resources are another way that the College remains ahead of the educational curve. These resources are often donated and supported by our partners in the business world, reflecting a unique relationship with industry that enables students to experience an educational environment where corporate partners share their expertise and exchange ideas with students and faculty.

Superlative Faculty

Southern California is a hotbed of innovation where the future is imagined and field-tested, and our distinguished faculty of more than 400 instructors is at the center of this vibrant community. Most of our faculty are working professionals—artists, photographers, painters, filmmakers and designers of every discipline—who are directly engaged with the demands of today's creative environment and bring their knowledge and fresh approaches into the studio. In addition to teaching the curriculum, our faculty members build relationships with students that last beyond the classroom.

Many of our faculty members are themselves Art Center alumni, reflecting the strong connection between the wider Art Center community and the College. In addition, our global alumni network of nearly 18,000 is a great resource for students, whether they are serving as mentors, presenting seminars or participating in special College projects.

Campus lectures, conferences and related events featuring the most influential thinkers—both within and outside the design world—expose students to an even broader mix of individuals whose ideas and actions are shaping not only design but society at large: scientists, engineers and entrepreneurs,

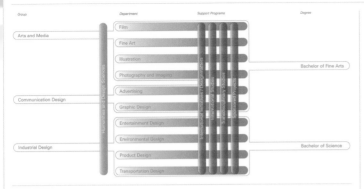

Group	Department	Support Programs	Degree
Arts and Media	Film		
	Fine Art		
	Illustration		
	Photography and Imaging		Bachelor of Fine Arts
Communication Design	Advertising		
	Graphic Design		
	Entertainment Design		
	Environmental Design		
Industrial Design	Product Design		Bachelor of Science
	Transportation Design		

The Cafeteria is the central gathering place where students can enjoy a meal, mingle with friends and faculty, study or just relax. Class lectures, meetings and events take place both inside the café and outside on the patio.

to name a few. Art Center's ability to attract the greatest minds across a variety of fields—our "third faculty"—sets us apart from other art and design colleges and benefits students in a number of ways, impacting their ideas, designs and conceptions of the creative individual's role within the wider context of society.

Whether it's through our superb faculty, inspiring alumni or brilliant guest speakers who expand the conversation beyond art and design, Art Center offers students a complete cycle of engagement unlike any other educational institution.

Preparing for the Future

The traditional lines once separating the art and design disciplines have blurred, transforming the creative world into a fluid environment where, for example, product designers collaborate with advertisers, and digital fine artists use the same computer software as graphic designers. With this fluidity comes a new professional freedom, as creative individuals increasingly navigate across disciplines during their professional lives.

At Art Center, we have designed a flexible curriculum that not only reflects this blurring of boundaries but also anticipates changes in the creative and business environments. Beginning with the first term, students receive comprehensive instruction in the foundation skills of their chosen discipline, ranging from drawing to three-dimensional fabrication. Rigorous research and instruction in a student's discipline is complemented by a broad spectrum of academic, creative and professional learning experiences.

Our organizational structure further encourages the sharing of ideas, experiences and problem-solving techniques among students and faculty. Art Center's core educational areas are represented by four broad groups—Arts and Media; Communication Design; Industrial Design; and Humanities and Design Sciences (see chart above). Through these groups, students are exposed to emerging trends in the field and are better equipped to apply that knowledge to their specific design discipline.

"Art Center's Student Government [ACSG] has been an invaluable asset to my college experience. When I joined ACSG, I found a group of people who were creative thinkers and wanted to make positive changes at Art Center. It changed everything for me—I met friends for life."—Traci Joy, Fine Art, eighth term

"There is no set path to becoming a creative leader. It is Art Center's mission as an educational institution to encourage and enable each student to develop his or her unique gifts and individuality, which is an essential component of professional, artistic and personal success."

—Richard Koshalek, President

Group: Arts and Media	Group: Communication Design	Group: Industrial Design
Film	*Advertising*	*Entertainment Design*
Fine Art	*Graphic Design*	*Environmental Design*
Illustration		*Product Design*
Photography and Imaging		*Transportation Design*

The James Lemont Fogg Memorial Library houses an unparalleled collection of print and online art and design reference materials, including 86,000 volumes of books and periodicals. The Library serves as an informal, collaborative learning environment, where students gather to do research, work on projects and study.

The fourth group, Humanities and Design Sciences, is the common thread running through each of the other groups, offering related liberal arts courses that enrich our students' studio work and help develop their critical thinking, problem solving and interpersonal skills.

Art Center's academic calendar simulates the pace and demands of a professional work environment and is comprised of three full terms each year. Students may complete the program in four years or

Film

A leading film executive recently commented: "What I like about the Art Center Film program is the understanding that movies aren't just shot, they're designed." Indeed, contemporary filmmaking demands a far broader range of skills than ever before. Digital tools now exist that can bring to life literally anything a filmmaker can imagine. The way viewers experience visual entertainment is also changing dramatically: motion pictures are created not just for movie theaters and television, but for computers and mobile devices as well.

Despite advances in technology and regardless of the size or location of the screen, a filmmaker must still be primarily a storyteller. Every aspect of Art Center's Film curriculum focuses on the mastery of moviemaking techniques in order to serve the narrative. Accomplished, working film professionals teach small, hands-on classes, fostering close mentoring relationships with students. Beginning with the first term, students immediately begin shooting in high definition video, eventually graduating to 35mm film. Students also enjoy an interdisciplinary curriculum exposing them to all of the visual arts related to contemporary filmmaking, while developing a deep foundation on the theory and history of filmmaking. This thorough education in the entire filmmaking process gives students the necessary skills and confidence to excel, whether they go on to work for a studio or network or on independent productions.

As the entertainment industry becomes more decentralized and diverse, filmmakers are increasingly required to function as leaders, visionaries and entrepreneurs as well as artists. Art Center's Film Department prepares students for success in these roles.

For course descriptions and faculty biographies, please visit artcenter.edu/catalog/film.

" Art Center trains filmmakers in both the art and craft of motion pictures—whether they're aimed for the theater screen, iPod screen or anything in between."

—Ross LaManna, Chair

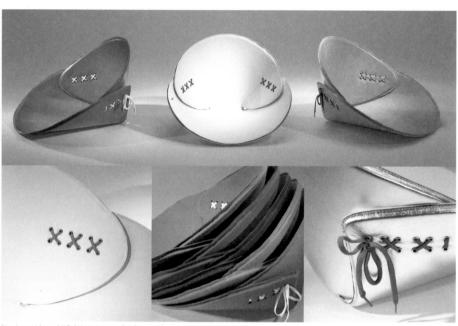

Aimee Less, eighth term. *Juki Flatfold* chair. Instructors: Cory Grosser and David Mocarski

"As a fine artist, I had always been interested in space, color and texture. I considered going back to school for interior design, but when I heard about Art Center's Environmental Design program, I became so excited. It seemed like a smarter approach to designing space . . . to think of the whole environment. I loved the Department's creative boundary-pushing attitude, and its promotion of design with a conscience and intellect."—Aimee Less

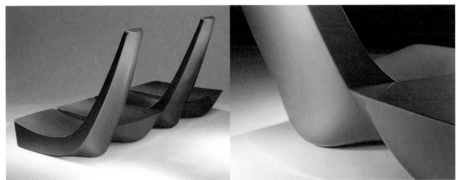

John Niero, sixth term. *J-Low.* Instructors: Cory Grosser and David Mocarski

John Niero, seventh term. *Beacon* satellite retail/event space. Instructor: Rob Ball

"My view on the role of design has broadened since coming to Art Center; I'm more honed in and focused. I think that the training and instruction that I've had here has really helped me further develop that focus." —John Niero

While the Art Center was redefining its mission and updating its identity, *Dot Magazine* was transformed from a bulletin covering college fundraising activities into a semiannual design journal. The first design decision was to change the format from a tabloid-sized, saddle-stitched magazine that was folded in half for mailing to a perfect-bound eight-by-ten-inch booklet with a heavy cover. Although previous covers were composed of photographs of school activities and plenty of type, the redesigned version of *Dot* always shows a detail of a student's work, which is also reproduced in full in the student portfolio section. To avoid detracting from the student's work, the only other elements on the cover are the publication's name, the college's logo, and the issue number. The name and logo remain in the same position from issue to issue, but the position of the issue number changes depending on the cover art. The color used for these elements also changes to harmonize with the cover image.

The inside was also reformatted. The magazine's departments— a spotlight section reporting on recent college developments and the student portfolio section—are treated consistently from issue to issue. The features—articles on current design issues relevant to both the Art Center and the wider design world—are treated like magazine editorials and are therefore designed to reflect their content. Some features have typography-driven layouts, some are photojournalistic or illustrative, and some are a combination of the two.

DOT Magazine 13

Art Center College of Design

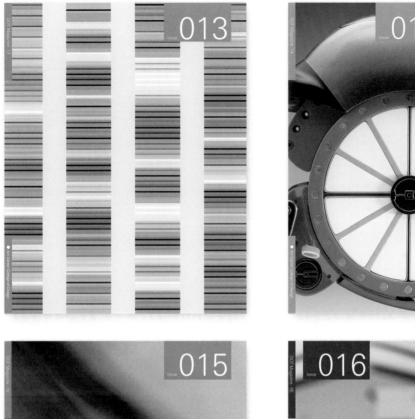

DOT Magazine 14

Art Center College of Design

DOT Magazine 15

Art Center College of Design

DOT Magazine 16

Art Center College of Design

ABCDEFGHI JKLMNOPQR STUVWXYZ

In 2004 Art Center established a biannual conference that convenes professionals not only from the design world but also from the arts, business, science, and other creative fields to discuss wide-ranging topics. Each conference has a broad theme meant to inspire thought and discussion among the speakers and participants. Themes such as "Stories from the Source" and "Radical Craft" are vague enough to allow the speakers to interpret them broadly and thus create a diverse array of presentations and ideas. Since the theme changes for every conference, the identity has to be very flexible. For the first conference, new letterforms were created to introduce the series as something brand-new for the college. This custom typeface was used on printed matter, signage, video projections, and other applications. Aside from the high caliber of the conference speakers, another attraction of the event is its location, Pasadena. The identities for each conference contain abundant vibrant colors meant to evoke sunny and bright California, but they are also graphic and nonspecific, in keeping with the abstract idea of each theme.

Conference program covers

|m|a|h|a|r|a|m|

Logo designs from the 1950s–1980s

Contract textiles are an indispensable part of the architecture and interior design fields, though there are few companies that manufacture textiles that provide superior design as well as function. While Maharam had consistently been a sales leader, it had never been perceived as offering well-designed products. Consequently, the company sought to update its identity and position itself as the leader in furnishing sophisticated design along with high-quality products.

Maharam dedicated itself to reviving textile patterns by modernist designers such as Charles and Ray Eames and Verner Panton as well as commissioning new textiles from leading contemporary artists and designers. The logotype and visual identity that were developed identify the company with twentieth-century design. The identity is built around Futura, a typeface closely associated with the Bauhaus and, therefore, with the architecture and design communities. The vertical lines positioned between the letters in the logotype are an abstract suggestion of fabric threads, the core of Maharam's business. The woven texture effect is not only a result of the placement of lines between the letters; it also arises from the contrast and repetition of the letters within the name Maharam, which is structured of alternating consonants and vowels. The letter *m* begins and ends the name; the letter *a* repeats three times, centered within the name; and the *h* and *r* are linked by shared visual attributes. The pattern of these letters imbues the logotype with visual symmetry. The geometric design of Futura letters contributes to the

|m|a|h|a|r|a|m|

251 Park Avenue South
New York, NY 10010

|m|a|h|a|r|a|m|

|m|a|h|a|r|a|m|

|m|a|h|a|r|a|m|

Michael Maharam
Principal

251
New Y

212.614.2
212.614.29
mmaharam@r

visual strength of the logotype. For example, the counterform of the *a*, which forms a dot, repeats three times in the logotype for an accentuated rhythm.

As part of the overhaul of its identity, Maharam launched an advertising campaign that featured the new logo but also pared down the information presented. A photograph of the product dominated most of the ads; the design and quality of the fabric were thought to be strong enough that little else was needed. The only type was the company logo, website address, phone number, and sometimes a short product description. Presenting a minimum of visual elements was in keeping with the minimalism and geometric simplicity of the new logotype.

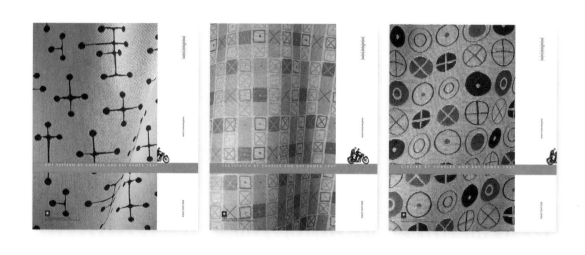

DOT PATTERN BY CHARLES AND RAY EAMES 1947

CROSSPATCH BY CHARLES AND RAY EAMES 1947

CIRCLES BY CHARLES AND RAY EAMES 1947

maharam

maharam.com

800.645.3943

FASHION TECHNOLOGY FOR SEATING

Bridging the gap between furniture and fashion, *Ready to Wear*
fuses form and surface to create integral upholstery solutions.

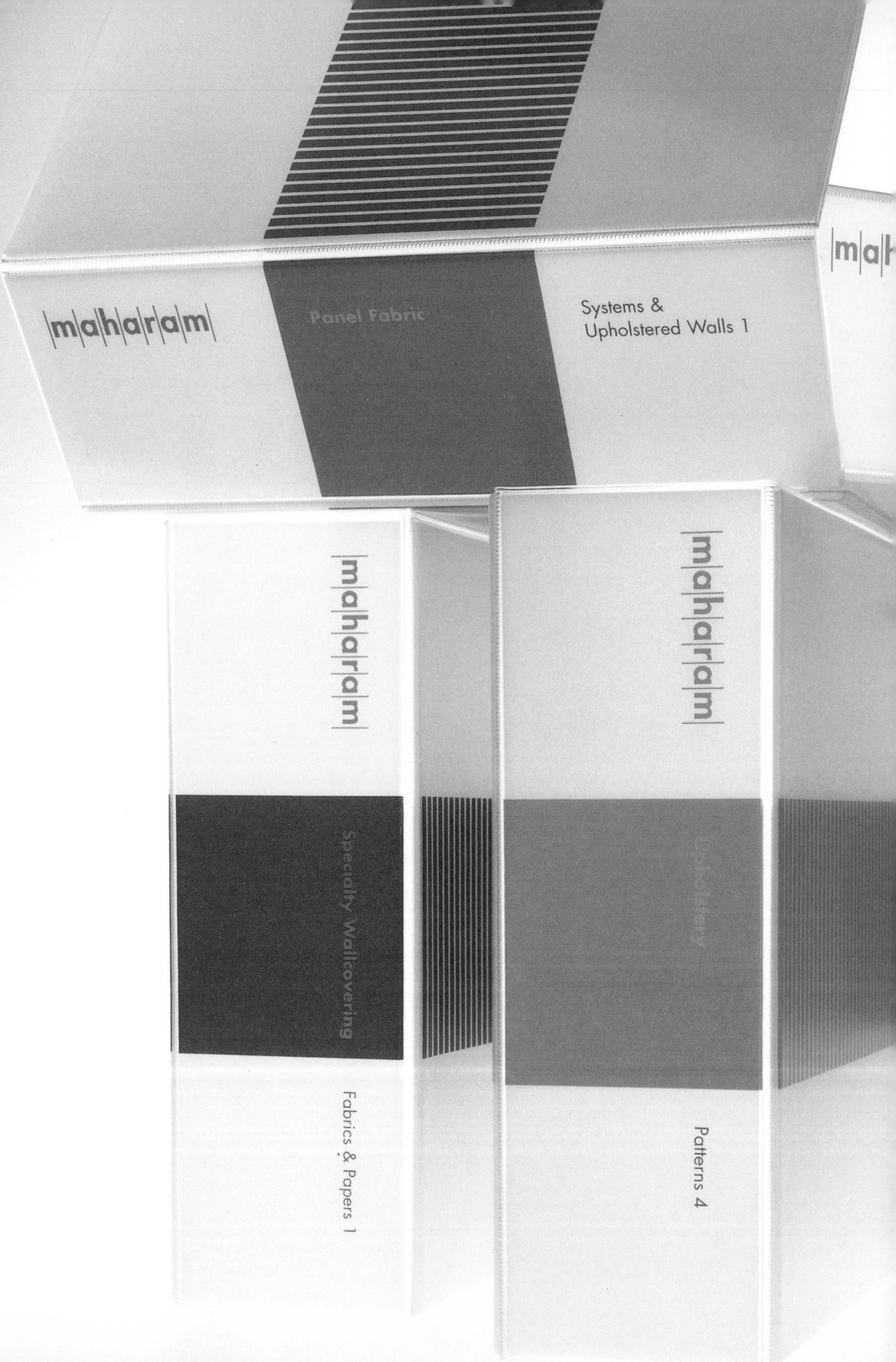

|maharam|

Panel Fabric

Systems &
Upholstered Walls 1

|ma

|maharam|

Specialty Wallcovering

Fabrics & Papers 1

|maharam|

Upholstery

Patterns 4

Duratex

Cubicle, Drapery, &
Bedspread Fabrics 1

|m|a|h|a|r|a|m|

Vinyl Wallcovering

Solids & Textures 1

This luxury hotel is located on Awashima, a tiny private island off the southern coast of central Japan with an unobstructed view of Mount Fuji. When he was building the resort in the 1980s, the client wanted to create a first-class, Western-style hotel—still a rarity in Japan at the time, especially outside major urban centers.

The hotel's spectacular view of Mount Fuji was an inspiration for the logo, a stylized depiction of the mountain with the waves of the Pacific Ocean lapping in the foreground. A zigzag shape, alluding to the cap of snow that almost always covers its peak, indicates the top of the mountain. The ocean's waves are symbolized by undulating horizontal lines, which also echo the zigzag. The logo's square shape allowed flexibility in its implementation. It was applied to all the signage and amenities, and it could also function as a pattern to be applied to other hotel items. In addition to the primary logo, a secondary logo was designed that consists simply of the horizontal wavy lines. *Yukatas*, lightweight cotton bathrobes, were printed with a pattern that alternates the primary and secondary logos. While it reinforces the hotel's identity, it is also a visually pleasing pattern in itself.

When the labels for the amenities, signage, and other elements of the branding system were designed, the type had to appear in both Japanese and English since the proprietors expected an international clientele. Copperplate, a display typeface designed by Frederic Goudy in 1901, was chosen for English. Characterized by its wide letters—almost every one

inhabits a square space rather than a narrow rectangle—Copperplate harmonizes with the Japanese type. Because most Japanese characters are wider than the letters of a typical Roman alphabet, the two different typefaces could have looked off-kilter, but Copperplate's blocky letters balance the Japanese characters even though the two alphabets look nothing alike.

Corporate brochure cover

The Japanese retail conglomerate Sazaby began in 1972 as a small company with one brand and fewer than fifty employees and by the 1990s had grown to a large corporation of many brands and several thousand employees. Sazaby specializes in lifestyle products, including clothing, accessories, home furnishings, food, and jewelry, primarily aimed at style-conscious, young Japanese women. Retail demands constant reassessment of the marketplace to maintain current, relevant product lines and to gauge competitors. Introducing new brands, product lines, and merchandise is crucial to keeping young customers interested, but Sazaby wanted a corporate identity distinct from the identities of its sub-brands. One reason was that the product lines were so diverse that one identity would not be suitable for all of them, but another important reason was that the company needed to allow for the possibility that some of the sub-brands would fail and it did not want failures to be associated with the parent company's name.

In creating the identities for the various sub-brands, the diversity of applications had to be taken into account. For example, the Afternoon Tea brand includes more than two thousand products and is also a chain of cafes. The logo for this brand had to be applied to shopping bags, sign-age, clothing, product tags, ceramics, linens, and menu covers. All the sub-brand logos were designed to translate well when applied to these different materials. Most had to be hand-drawn so that the type would remain crisp and legible when they were greatly enlarged or reduced.

AfternoonTea

VIASAZABY

Creating a logotype always presents a challenge to the designer because of the brevity of its form. To be effective, a logotype must be concise and instantly comprehensible. The viewer should be able to understand immediately what the logo is designed to communicate. Color and typography are central components of logotype design. Although the mark or symbol is often perceived to be the essence of a logo, its application will also determine what the logo communicates. Printing and fabrication methods can influence the look of an identity system and thereby how the people behind the name are represented. While conventional offset printing is sufficient for applying almost any logotype, a design can be enhanced by such techniques as letterpress printing, engraving, and embossing, all of which can increase the tactile quality of printed materials. Fluorescent inks, metallic inks, and hot stamps can amplify the visual impact of a logotype.

Opposite: Eyebeam; page 56: Merrill C. Berman Collection; page 57: DimsonHomma; page 58: Bendheim; page 59: Pen Plus Inc.; page 60: I Pezzi Dipinti; page 61: Sugimoto Studio

ROBERT HOMMA

RISE DIMSON

DIMSONHOMMA
20 EAST 67TH STREET, NEW YORK, N.Y. 10021
TELEPHONE 212.439.7950   FACSIMILE 212.439.7960

SUGIMOTO STUDIO

HIROSHI SU

508 WE

NEW Y

[T] 2

[F]

Chaise longue, designed by Richard
Meier for Knoll International, 1982

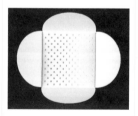

Holiday card with die-cut envelope

These four pieces illustrate the design possibilities that the die cut offers.
The announcement of the architect Richard Meier's furniture designs
for Knoll International (above) uses the die cut to conceal and reveal
information, creating a surprise for the viewer. Meier, known for his spare,
elegant designs, created a furniture collection based on a grid made up of
squares, and all the pieces were produced in only black or white. For the
invitation to the collection's debut, the die cut was employed to hint at
the furniture's design. Vertical columns were cut out of the first panel
of the three-panel card; the middle panel is identical except that it is
rotated ninety degrees. Neither of these two panels contains type. When
folded, the two panels overlap to form a grid of squares. The recipient
opens the envelope to find a white square card with no visible printing.
When the card is open, the recipient sees the type on the third panel.
The middle panel is printed solid black, as is the reverse side of the first
panel, so when the first two panels are held closed in the left hand as the
recipient reads the third panel, a black grid appears that is identical to
the white grid one sees when the card is closed.

In a holiday card for Knoll (right and below left), the custom-made
square envelope opens on all four sides and looks like a flower when laid
flat. Once open, the envelope reveals a card that is all white, with no type
on the front. The front of the card is dotted with a grid of die-cut holes.
The recipient opens the card to find *Happy Holidays* engraved in gold
in the spaces between the holes. The effect is quiet and elegant, and

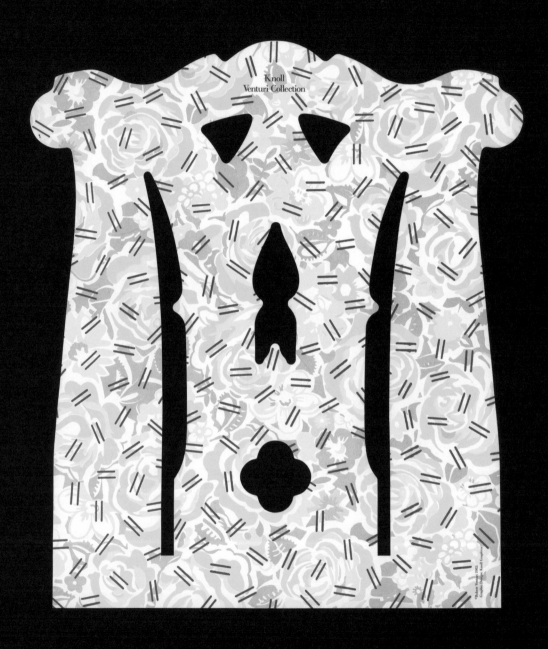

Knoll
Venturi Collection

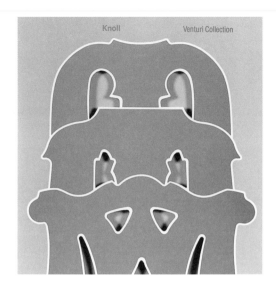

both the holes and the loosely kerned type bring to mind the falling snow of the winter holidays.

When the architect Robert Venturi designed a furniture collection for Knoll, he took classic historical furniture styles—Queen Anne, Chippendale, Empire—and radically simplified their silhouettes, flattening them and exaggerating their proportions. The chairs he designed were constructed of molded laminated plywood, a technique devised by Alvar Aalto in the early 1930s, so from the side the chairs have a very flat profile. The silhouette of one of the chair backs was used to create a poster (left) to announce the debut of the collection. The chair back was reproduced at its actual size, a die cut used to describe its contours. The chair chosen for the announcement was also printed in a pattern that Venturi designed. Some of the posters were left flat, but for the invitation (below right) the poster was folded in ninths and inserted into a custom-made square envelope (the same envelope that was used for the holiday card) along with a sheet of vellum that was printed with the details of the event. A sixteen-page, saddle-stitched product brochure (above) showed the collection in full. The cover, which again employed a die cut to show the silhouettes of the chair backs, was an eight-page gatefold. The second and third panels were die cut to show the contours of the chair backs and printed in two solid grays. The insides of the first and last panels were printed in a solid pale green, so the cover is purely flat and decorative, alluding to the flatness of the plywood chairs.

Round dining table with urn base and "Chippendale" chairs, both with "Grandmother's Tablecloth" laminate, designed by Robert Venturi for Knoll International, 1984

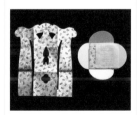

Invitation for the introduction of the Venturi Collection

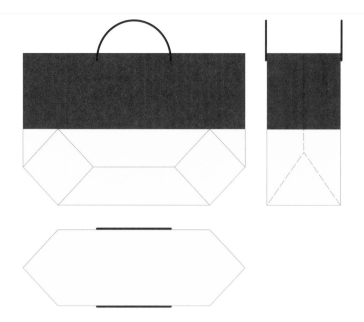

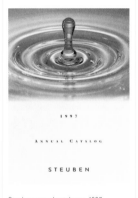

Steuben annual catalogue, 1997

The American glassmaker Steuben required a shopping bag that reflected the luxury of its products and was sturdy enough to hold them. Modeled after the shape of the sacks used for collecting apples at orchards, the bag is identical to an ordinary brown paper shopping bag, but the folding was altered in order to make the outside of the bag wider. Instead of the gussets on the sides folding inward, as they do on most shopping bags, they fold outward. This simple modification created more space for printing on the outside of the bag, which Steuben saw as a benefit because the shopping bag can act as a moveable billboard to advertise the brand. The trapezoidal shape also sets it apart from most other shopping bags. Because Steuben's products are solid glass, some of the largest pieces weigh more than ten pounds and require an extra-sturdy bag. Very heavy paper was chosen, and covering it with a matte laminate strengthened it. The cotton string handles are extra-thick to bear the weight of heavy boxes.

Robert Isabell, the florist and event planner known for his impeccable style, launched a product line in 1996 that included perfumes and scented bath products and candles. Isabell wanted very clean and modern packaging, breaking away from the frilly and feminine look of most beauty and perfume packaging at that time. He also wanted everything to be manufactured in the United States. For the perfume bottles, a clear test tube was the starting point. A New Jersey manufacturer of laboratory-grade glass produced the cylindrical bottles, which were of uniform thickness throughout. The color of each perfume became a design element; when the bottles were full, they looked like columns of pure color and the thin walls of the bottle were barely visible. The dipsticks were made of the same glass, which was also unusual. Usually, dipsticks are made of inexpensive plastic because they are often an afterthought and not part of the package design, but Isabell wanted the dipstick to be perfectly straight, echoing the straight silhouette of the bottle. It was also important for it to be straight because the only adornment on the bottle was the perfume name. The dipstick had to align with the columnar type and not detract from the symmetry of bottle and type. The only way to achieve that was to make it from glass, as a plastic stick would curve to one side and mar the visual balance of the package.

A simple metal electrical wiring box was the inspiration for the perfume box. The original idea was to construct the entire box, including the tray that held the perfume bottle, from aluminum, but that proved to be too expensive. Also, if the tray were metal, it would scratch the aluminum bottle top. Instead, the bottom of the box and the tray were made of aluminum-colored paper, and the box top was made of brushed aluminum. Two sides of the top were left open to make fabrication simpler and less expensive. The Minnesota manufacturer produced items for the automobile industry and was capable of etching the type on the box top with a diamond cut, which gave the letters a subtle sparkle and made them pop from the surface of the matte aluminum.

The hexagonal candle packages stood apart from the many other candles on the market, most of which came in standard square boxes. Like the perfumes, the candles were packaged in simple clear glass cylinders. Each scent was given a different color, and each box was printed with a solid muted color to indicate the color of the candle inside.

Beaker and aluminum electrical box (top);

early package prototype (bottom)

Early sketch

In the early 1980s the design store Sointu, one of the first to specialize in objects as designs in and of themselves, opened on East Sixty-ninth Street in New York City. Sointu commissioned various designers to create watches. The components of a watch are few—strap, face, hands, and markings to denote hours—and it is difficult to invent new treatments of them. Each watch in this group of eleven was treated in one of three ways: manipulating the crystal, giving the face or hands a graphic treatment, or exploring the surface texture of the face. On several watches, the crystal was sandblasted to give it a frosted appearance. On some of these, the sandblasted areas (or the voids left around them) became the markings for the hours. Numbers were not used for the markings on any of the watches; the hours were indicated by squares, circles, triangles, and, in one case, hash marks. Simple graphic treatments were applied to some of the watch faces: horizontal lines covered the face of one and the numbers were denoted by interruptions in the linear pattern. On another, the two hands were shaped so that they formed the silhouette of the Empire State building when they converged. For a new surface treatment, metal painted with a pebbly, slightly sparkly surface was used.

A.S.A.P.

The Acadia Summer Arts Program, or A.S.A.P., is a summer residency program located in Acadia National Park, on Mount Desert Island, Maine. For more than fifteen years, an ever-expanding group of artists, poets, curators, architects, dancers, and other arts professionals has been gathering in Acadia to take advantage of the breathtaking natural landscape and the opportunity to mingle with a diverse group of creative people. The island is dotted with private cottages that guests are free to use as either peaceful workspaces or for simple rest and relaxation. The logo intimates the landscape setting: the letters symbolize the hills and pine trees and the periods represent the lakes and ponds dotted throughout the island. The first version of the stationery was based on the fall colors of Acadia—ocher, deep blue, dark green, and maroon. In subsequent versions the colorways were altered to reflect impressions of the landscape at different times of the year. The identity was applied not only to stationery but also to T-shirts, hats, bags, and even mailboxes.

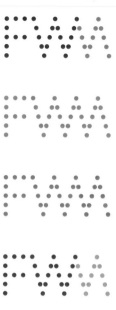

The Fabric Workshop and Museum, a nonprofit arts organization in Philadelphia, began in 1977 as a craft-oriented enterprise focused on producing textiles in collaboration with artists. It has since developed into a full-fledged fine-art "laboratory" and museum. The institution offers residencies for artists to create ambitious, often large-scale works and employs a staff of experienced artists and craftspeople to aid in their execution.

Preparing to celebrate its twenty-fifth anniversary, in 2004, the Fabric Workshop decided to revise its identity in order to reflect its maturity and expanded role in the fine-art community. The new visual identity had to communicate its roots as an arts collective as well as its new position as a permanent institution of art production and guardianship.

A survey of arts organizations was conducted to review the visual identities of other institutions. In order to create a stronger and more memorable identity, the abbreviation FWM was chosen for the logo rather than the full name. In some typefaces, the letters *M* and *W* are mirror images, a fact that was taken into consideration when designing the logo. The *W* and the *M* merge and are indicated in two colors. Their zigzag shape suggests sewing and intimates the institution's origins as a textile workshop. Various color combinations were developed so that the color of the logo can change, depending on whether it is applied to advertisements, signage, invitations, or other promotional materials. Four different color combinations were applied to the components of the

The Fabric Workshop and Museum
1315 Cherry Street, 5ᵗʰ Floor
Philadelphia, PA 19107

Marion Boulton Stroud
Founder/Artistic Director

The Fabric Workshop and Muse
1315 Cherry Street, 5ᵗʰ Floor
Philadelphia, PA 19107
[T] 215.568.1111 ext. 22 [F] 215.568.
kippyss@fabricworkshopandmuseum
www.fabricworkshopandmuseum.org

stationery system. One color combination was printed on the outside of the envelope and a different one was printed on the letterhead. A special set of stationery was produced for the museum director. On these stationery components the logo was laser die cut into the paper instead of printed. The letterhead, second sheet, and business cards were also printed with a solid color—either red or magenta—on the back.

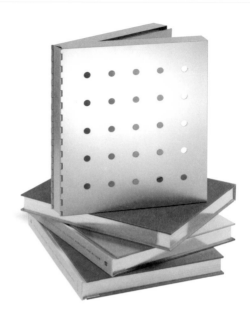

NEW MATERIAL
AS NEW MEDIA:
THE FABRIC
WORKSHOP
AND MUSEUM

Cover design for trade edition

Published on the occasion of the Fabric Workshop and Museum's twenty-fifth anniversary, this catalogue presents some of the most significant projects created at the institution. Its founder and artistic director wanted the publication to be celebratory and memorable, so there was wide latitude it its design. The primary concept was to approach the catalogue as a three-dimensional object. Every surface was treated to transform it from an everyday book into an object. Instead of reproducing an artwork on the cover, a lustrous bookbinding cloth that was available in vibrant colors was used. The front cover, back cover, and spine were each wrapped in a different colored cloth. Three different covers were designed, so nine colors were used. To use three different fabrics per book, a special binding was devised. The spine, front cover, and back cover were all wrapped separately then assembled. The only place type appears is on the spine. For the trade edition, a clear acetate jacket was designed; the front of the jacket was printed with silver type so the reader can see the colors of the cover through it. Before the book was bound, the edges of the pages were gilded in silver leaf. No plain white paper is visible, which also helps to transform it into a unique object. For a special edition, a piano-hinged case was constructed of brushed aluminum and die-cut with twenty-five holes on the front to signify the twenty-fifth anniversary.

STROUD   NEW MATERIAL AS NE

STROUD   NEW MATERIAL AS N

STROUD   NEW MATERIAL AS N

Tom Friedman

About the artist

American, born 1965, lives in Northampton, Massachusetts

Tom Friedman lives in rural Western Massachusetts. He completed
a BFA in graphic illustration at Washington University in St. Louis
(1988), before going on to earn an MFA in sculpture from the
University of Illinois at Chicago (1990). Since 1995, when the
Museum of Modern Art, New York, featured Friedman's work in their
Projects series, he has been the focus of many solo exhibitions,
including a major show organized by the Southeastern Center for
Contemporary Arts in Winston-Salem, NC (2000), which traveled to
the Museum of Contemporary Art in Chicago, the Yerba Buena Center
for the Arts in San Francisco, and the New Museum of Contemporary
Art in New York, among other venues. In 1993 he was awarded The
Louis Comfort Tiffany Foundation Award.

About the work

Tom Friedman's *Untitled* project, created with the FW+M, is the most recent of his
self-portraits. Earlier endeavors have included a carving of his face on an aspirin pill
and a full-body sculpture measuring five inches and carved from a block of Styrofoam.

Taken from a passport-size photograph, Friedman's FW+M collaboration is based
on a mathematical formula by which 256 copies of this image were duplicated, dissected
and re-configured to create an abstracted photographic self-portrait. Friedman used
a similar technique to create two previous projects—a U.S. one-dollar bill and a cereal
box. The images were cut into 33,072 1/4-inch squares based on a series of nearly
imperceptible 1/64-inch deviations. One by one, they were then assembled to create a
magnified, out-of-focus mosaic of the original self-portrait.

Friedman has said of the complexity involved in fabricating his work that it arises
partly from his "inability to process everything that I'm confronted with and the idea of
the whole . . . What unifies what I do is the phenomenon of taking something that is
crystal clear to me, something I seem to know, and finding that the closer I get and the
more carefully I inspect it, the less clear it becomes" (*Tom Friedman*, Phaidon Press
Limited, London, 2001).

Untitled, 2001 (detail). Photographs, museum board, and adhesive. 60 x 40 inches (152.4 x 101.6 cm). Private collection.

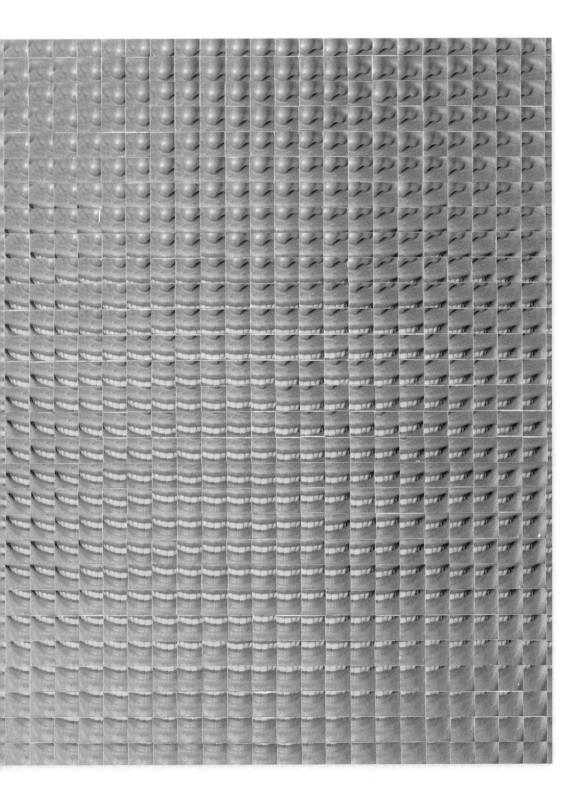

Passport photograph used to create *Untitled*, 2001 (above). 2 x 3 inches (5.08 x 7.62 cm).

Untitled, 2001 (right). Photographs, museum board, and adhesive. 60 x 40 inches (152.4 x 101.6 cm).

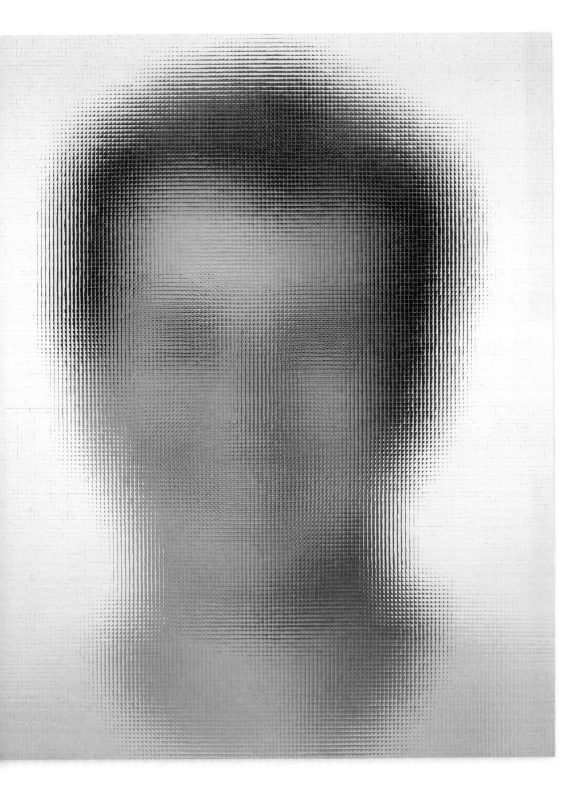

Industrial Strength Sleep on the loom at
Flanders Tapestries, Wielsbeke, Belgium

This small catalogue documented an exhibition at the Fabric Workshop and Museum by the artist Ed Ruscha. The FWM commissioned Ruscha, best known for his paintings that combine words and images, to create a new work for the 2007 installation. He took one of his own paintings, *Industrial Strength Sleep* (1989), and replicated it at a larger size as a tapestry. Both the original painting and the new tapestry were exhibited. The challenge in reproducing the works in the catalogue was that they are both very large. The painting is five-by-twelve feet and the tapestry is nearly nine-by-twenty-two feet. When both were reduced to fit on the book page, their differences were almost indistinguishable: neither the brushstrokes of the painting nor the texture of the woven tapestry was visible. In order to communicate the tapestry's tactile quality, it was reproduced at three different sizes in the plate section. A full-page spread shows the entire tapestry, the next spread shows an enlarged portion of the center, and the last shows a close-up photograph of a small piece. Only in the last reproduction can the viewer see that the work is made of fabric because the woven threads are evident at this scale. For the jacket, end leaves, and divider pages, different parts of the tapestry were photographed at close range and reproduced at one-to-one scale to increase the viewer's sense of the work's texture and depth.

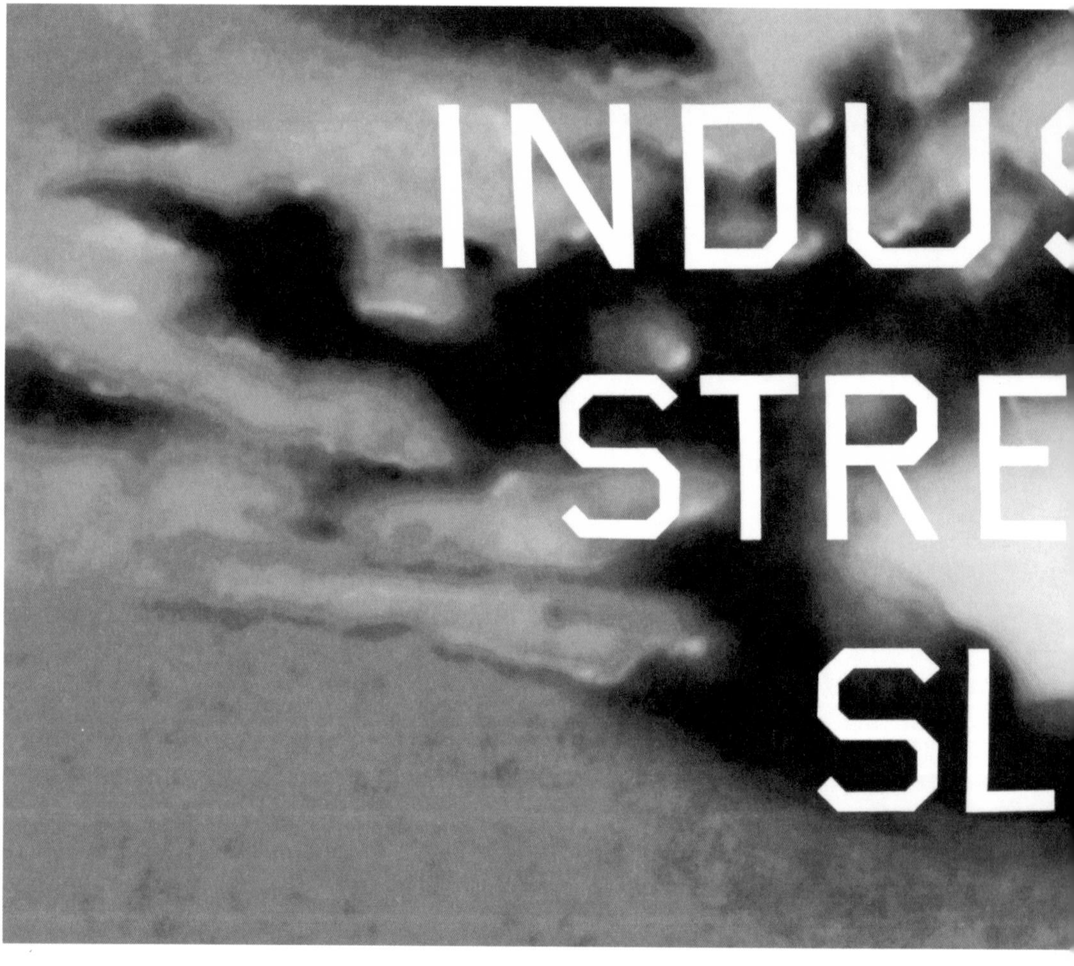
INDUS
STRE
SL

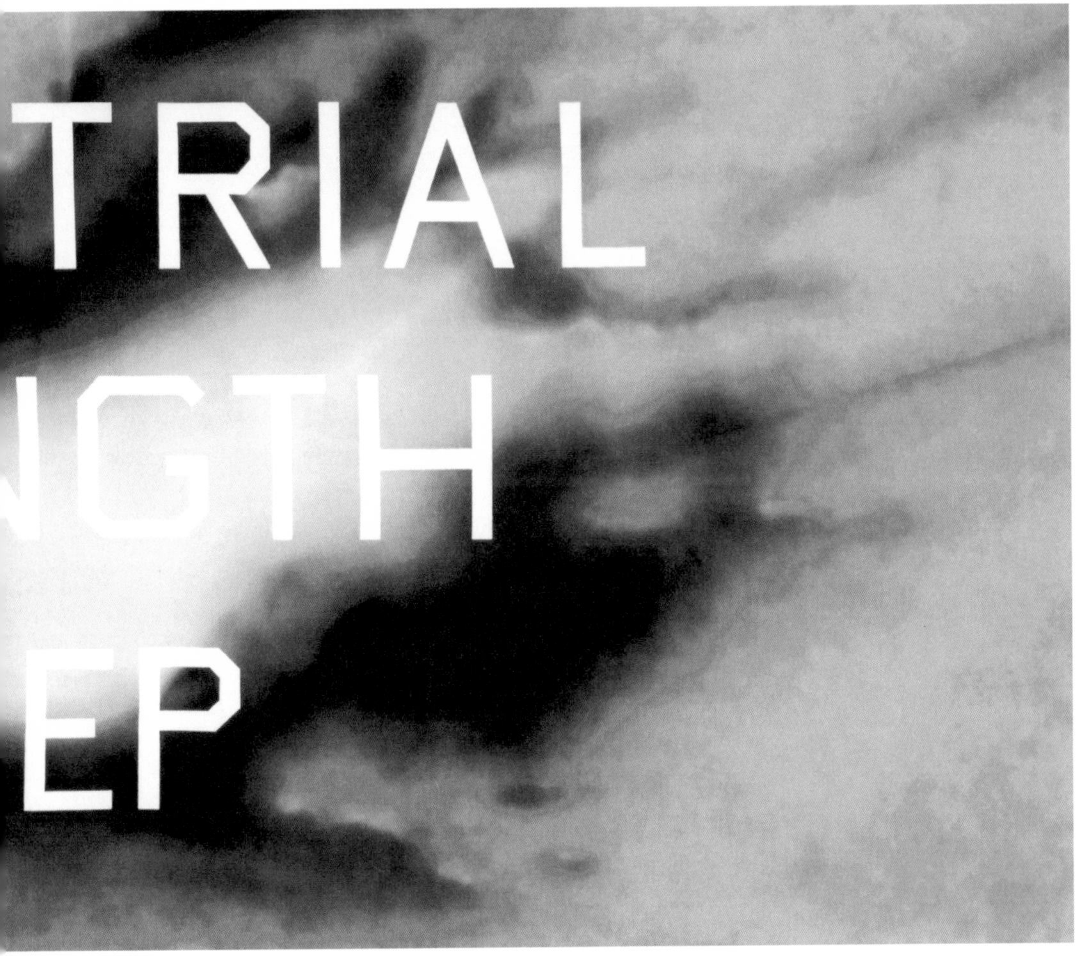
TRIAL
NGTH
EP

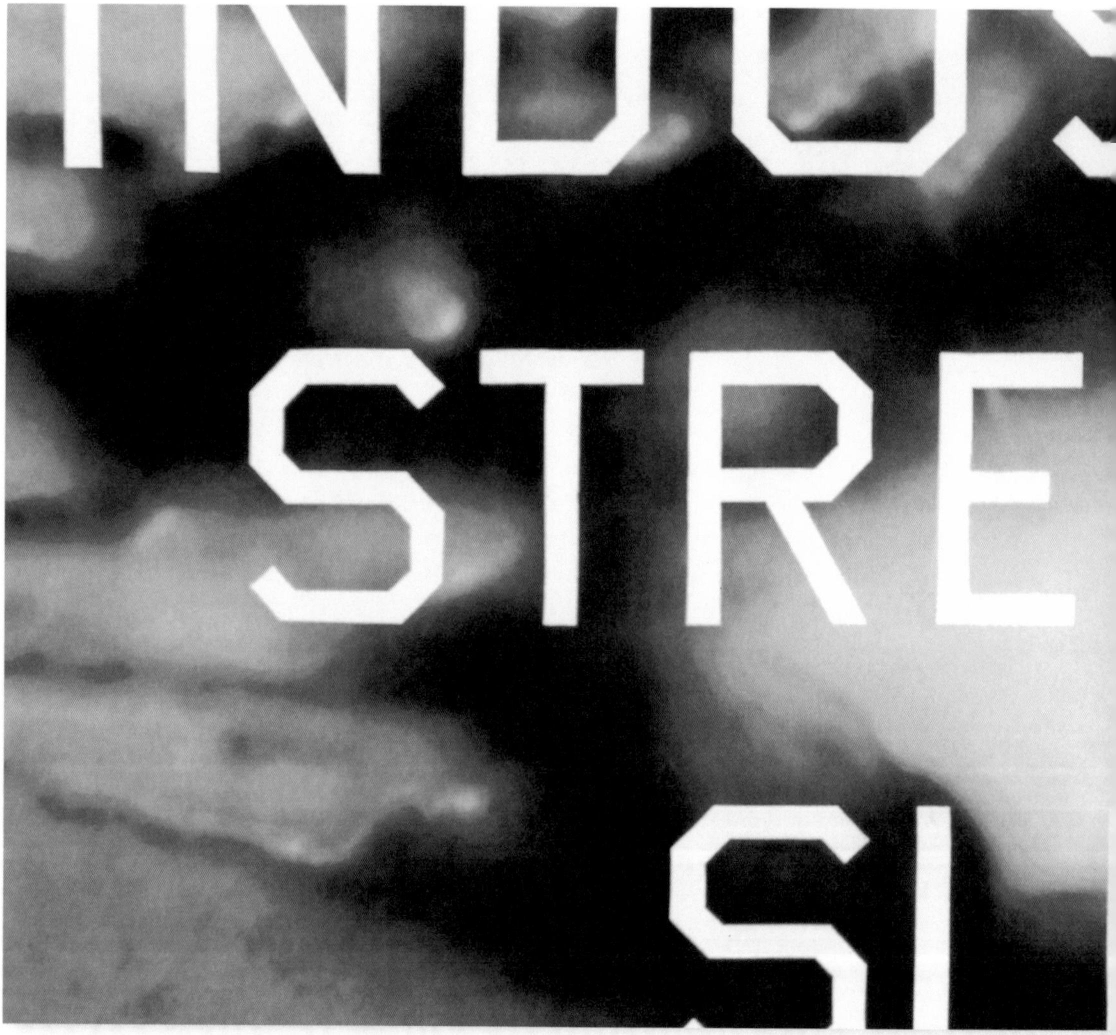
INDUS
STRE

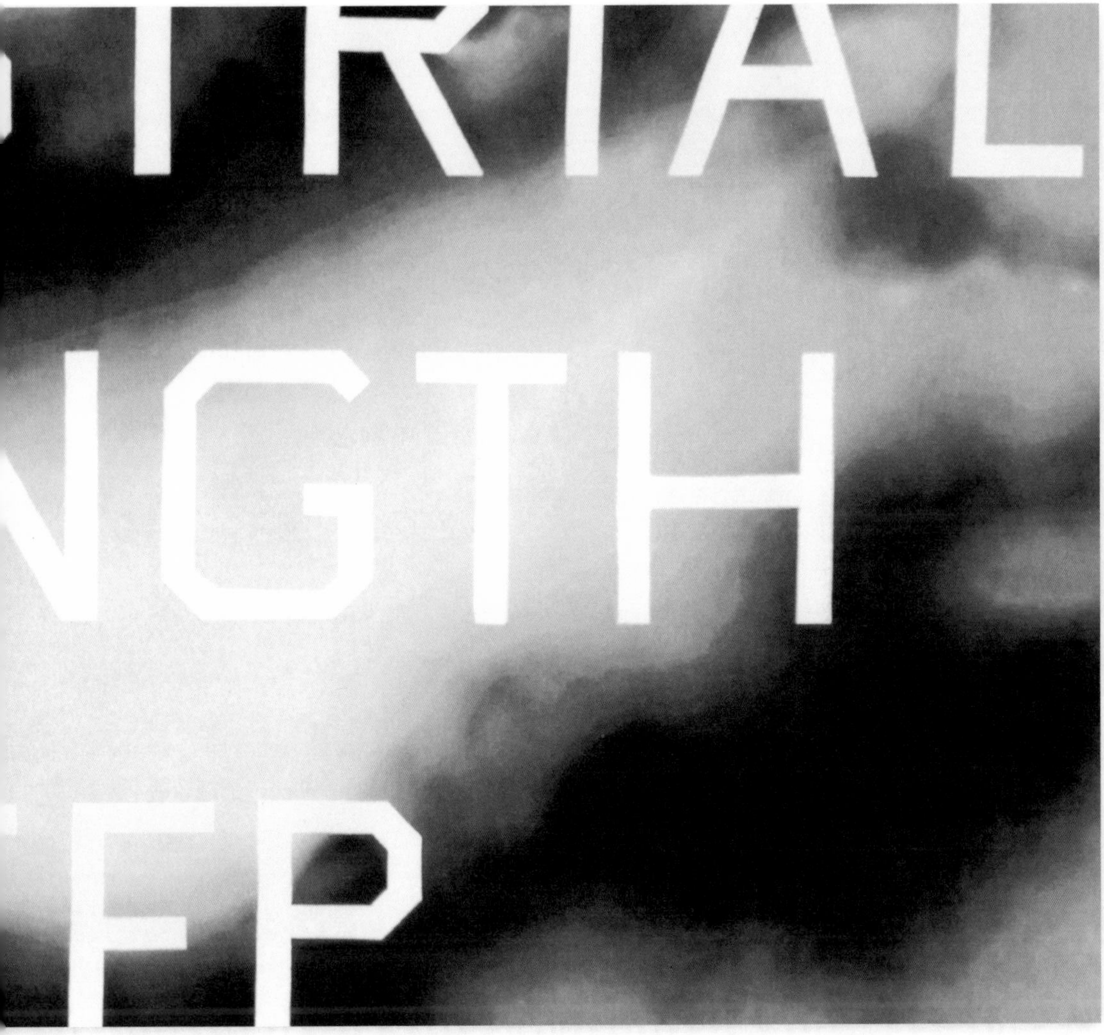
TRIAL
NGTH

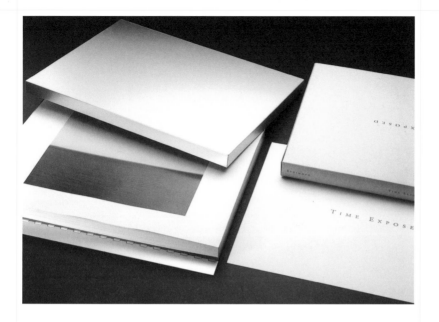

Time Exposed is a limited-edition portfolio of fifty black-and-white photo-graphs of seascapes from around the world by the artist Hiroshi Sugimoto. Only one thousand copies were published. The photographs were printed tritone on an offset printer. Each photograph was trimmed then hand-tipped on a heavy, uncoated rag mounting paper embossed with the area the image occupies. The name, date, and negative number of the artwork were also blind embossed on the bottom of the sheet, so the type does not detract from the photograph. Rather than binding the pages together, as in a conventional book, a brushed-aluminum case was designed to house the loose sheets. This treatment emphasizes that the work inside is fine art. The top of the custom-made case is closed on all four sides and slides over the bottom of the case. A piano hinge was built into one of the two long sides of the case bottom. The hinge flips down so that the folios can be taken out or put in the case easily and without damage. A cardboard slipcase both protects the case from scratches and provides space for displaying the title, since there is no printing on the case.

Installation view, "Time Exposed,"
Carnegie Museum of Art, Pittsburgh, 1991

From the 1970s through the 1990s the artist Hiroshi Sugimoto created a series of photographs of American movie theaters. Each exposure was timed to last the duration of the movie being shown when he took the photograph. In the resulting artworks, a detailed image of the theater's interior (or the landscape surrounding the drive-ins that he photographed) emerged, while the image of the screen was rendered completely blank.

The original gelatin-silver prints contain subtle gradations of gray and black. The dry-trap process—printing one color at a time and allowing the ink to dry between runs—was employed using four colors—black and three grays—to print the reproductions for the catalogue *Theaters: Hiroshi Sugimoto*. With this technique, Sugimoto's photographs were reproduced as close to the originals as possible. Applying the ink in stages creates crisper dots that bleed into one another less than they do in conventional offset printing, allowing for finer detail. The dry-trap method requires a one-color press, and at the time the book was printed there was only one press operator at the printing plant with the skill and experience to run it. Since the registration must be adjusted each time a new color is printed, it is not possible to see all four colors at once until the final color is being printed. Adjustments to the ink density must be made based on intuition and experience.

Uncoated paper was used for greater ink saturation, which, when coupled with the dry-trap technique, also contributed to enhanced detail and depth in the photographs. The cover and the end leaves were

Step 1

Step 2

Step 3

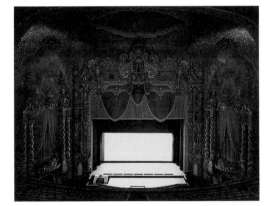

Step 4

silk-screened with Day-Glo ink and matte film laminated to re-create
the illusion of light captured in the photographs. A special edition
of the publication was accompanied by a limited edition of Sugimoto's
U.A. Walker, New York (1978) photogravure. One thousand prints were
numbered and signed by the artist and cased in a custom-made, piano-
hinged, brushed-aluminum box.

UNION CITY DRIVE-IN, UNION CITY, 1993

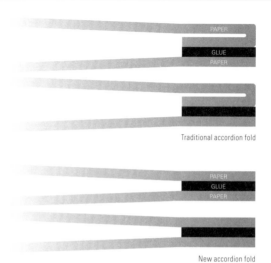

Traditional accordion fold

New accordion fold

This limited-edition book contains a series of sixty photographs by Sugimoto taken at the Sanju-sangen-do temple in Kyoto. The twelfth-century temple houses 1,001 statues of the Buddha arranged in rows along one of its long walls. The photographs were printed on sixty sheets of paper glued together accordion-fold style, resulting in 120 pages. Test prints were done on both coated and uncoated papers, but the coated papers cracked when they were scored for the fold, marring the photographs. The uncoated papers did not crack and also had the benefit of adding bulk to the book. The accordion fold for *Sea of Buddha* differs from most in that the seams were not folded inward and then glued; instead, the backs of the pages were glued together, which kept the book from getting bulky at the edges. A standard gluing technique would have made the thickness of the book uneven. The pages do not open perfectly flat, as with a normal accordion fold, so the viewer flips through page by page rather than opening the book to view the photos all at once. Because of the accordion fold there is no spine, so traditional binding was not possible. The front and back covers are made of brushed aluminum glued directly to the first and last pages. Without a spine, the book can easily be damaged, so a slipcase is necessary to protect it. The slipcase is covered in khaki-colored silk.

Sugimoto's photographs of important twentieth-century architecture in this catalogue for the 2003 exhibition "Sugimoto: Architecture" at the Museum of Contemporary Art, Chicago, were all made in soft focus, which gives the subjects an enigmatic quality, even though most of the buildings—such as the Guggenheim Museum and the Chrysler building—are well known. To emphasize the aura of mystery that the photographs impart, a detail was reproduced on the jacket, creating an abstract, geometric image. Many different papers were tested before the final jacket was designed. Most of the vellums were brittle and cracked where the jacket was scored, but a translucent paper made entirely of plastic proved to be pliable enough to bend and not crack or tear.

A smaller version of the original exhibition traveled to the Art Center College of Design (the artist's alma mater). The special invitation for this venue was designed as a poster; the photograph was reproduced on one side and the information about the exhibition was on the reverse. It was printed on light newsprint so it could be folded into sixteenths, making it an appropriate size for mailing. Some were printed on heavier paper and left flat so they could be given away as commemorative posters.

Installation view, "Sugimoto: Architecture," Museum of Contemporary Art, Chicago, 2003

Folded self-mailer invitation on newsprint

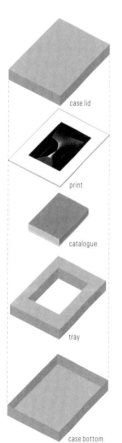

case lid

print

catalogue

tray

case bottom

This catalogue was published to accompany the 2005–6 late-career retrospective "Hiroshi Sugimoto" at the Mori Art Museum, Tokyo, and the Hirshhorn Museum and Sculpture Garden, Washington, D.C. Most of Sugimoto's photography is black and white, though there are some color photographs in the plate section and the contributors used color illustrations for their essays. There were thus two kinds of printing for the inside of the book: most of the plates were printed tritone (black and two grays), and the essay section and one signature of the plate section were printed using the standard four-color process. The pages had to be organized so that each sixteen-page signature included only black and white or color. Including both types of reproductions in the same signature would have required printing seven colors at once (cyan, magenta, yellow, black, two grays, and a varnish)—more than the press could accommodate. The only type is on the spine, and the only thing on the cover is a detail of a seascape.

Sugimoto made twenty-five prints of two different photographs to accompany a limited edition of fifty volumes. The special edition was housed in a custom-made brushed-aluminum box and tray. The box was designed to accommodate the mounted print, which was larger than the book. An aluminum tray nested inside the box, and the book was placed inside the tray. The height of the tray was determined by the book's thickness so that the book lay flush with the top of the tray. The print was then placed on top of the book, and the box was closed with the unadorned aluminum lid.

KERRY BROUGHER AND DAVID ELLIOTT

HIROSHI SUGIMOTO

CATALOGUE DESIGNED BY TAKAAKI MATSUMOTO

HIRSHHORN MUSEUM AND SCULPTURE GARDEN
SMITHSONIAN INSTITUTION
WASHINGTON, D.C.

MORI ART MUSEUM, TOKYO

IN ASSOCIATION WITH
HATJE CANTZ PUBLISHERS

56

CALIFORNIA CONDOR, 1994

GOLDEN EAGLE, 1994

Richard Serra. *Joe*, 2000. Weathering
steel. Installtion view at the Pulitzer
Foundation for the Arts, Saint Louis

Joe features the work of the sculptor Richard Serra, the photographer Hiroshi Sugimoto, and the writer Jonathan Safran Foer. Serra was commissioned to create a sculpture for the Pulitzer Foundation for the Arts, and his torqued spiral of weathered steel, *Joe*, sits permanently outside the Pulitzer building in Saint Louis. On a trip to the foundation in 2003, Sugimoto intended to photograph the Tadao Ando–designed building but instead was drawn to the Serra sculpture. Taken from various vantage points within the sculpture, the photographs are characterized by large, abstract shapes created by the intersection of sky, steel, and grass. When the Pulitzer Foundation expressed interest in publishing a book on the series, Sugimoto thought another layer of artistic experience could be added with an original text by a novelist, so Foer was invited. The monumental sculpture is more than thirteen feet high and forty-eight feet wide, and Sugimoto's photographs of it are correspondingly large, 58 ¾ by 47 inches. The trim size of the book is also large to reflect the scale of both artists' work. To determine the largest size feasible, the first factor was the binding. The width of the book is the maximum that can be accommodated by a European machine binder. A book any larger would have to be hand-bound, which is prohibitively expensive. Although the photographs are impressionistic and not documentary, the layout of the pages gives the reader the impression of walking through the sculpture. Foer's text was treated like poetry and set in the center of each page.

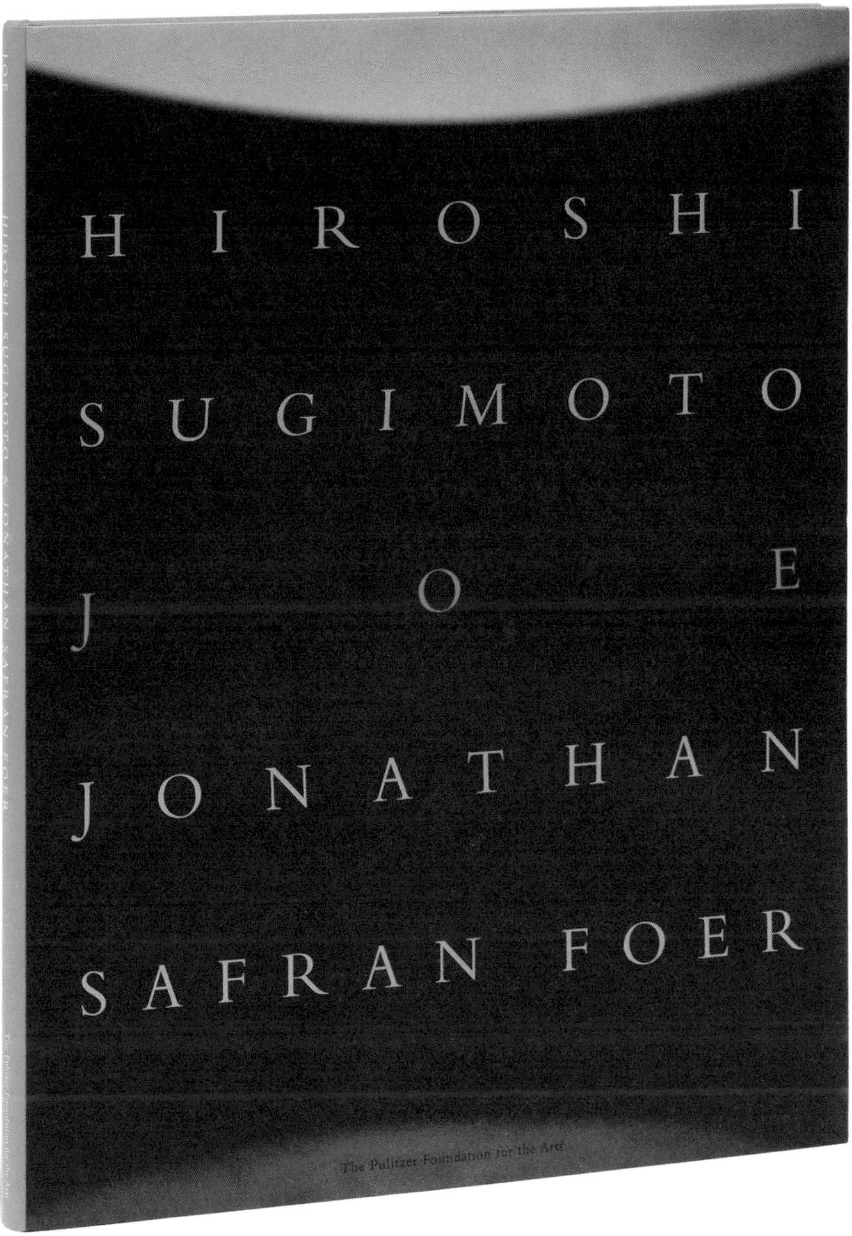

HIROSHI

SUGIMOTO

J   O   E

JONATHAN

SAFRAN FOER

The Pulitzer Foundation for the Arts

With a fishing line,

Joe sews shut the pockets of his jacket.

It's his favorite jacket,

because it has so many pockets—

four on each side of the chest.

WILD FASHION UNTAMED

THE METROPOLITAN MUSEUM OF ART

The abundance of fur, feathers, and animal skins in the 2004–5 exhibition "Wild: Fashion Untamed" at the Metropolitan Museum of Art encouraged the use of unconventional materials and processes for the book. The exhibition catalogue is smaller than most—only 9 ⅞ by 6 ⅞ inches. One reason for choosing this size is that digital photographs from fashion runway shows or editorial spreads in fashion magazines are often too small to be greatly enlarged without suffering a loss in quality. The high-gloss paper used makes the reproductions jump off the page and gives the book a racy feel, in keeping with the subject.

The cover presented an opportunity to use unusual materials. A lizard-patterned, opalescent paper was selected, and a sharkskin-patterned paper was used for the end leaves. The jacket image is a Bert Stern photograph of a woman in profile, her face in heavy white makeup, wearing a multicolored snakeskin hood. If the jacket were printed on a standard opaque sheet, the lizard-print cover would be visible only at the top and bottom edges of the book. To make the patterned cover more visible, a clear acetate sheet was tried for the jacket. The model's face was silhouetted and the rest of the jacket was left blank. The lizard-skin paper, visible through the unprinted parts of the jacket, was so strong that it competed with the snakeskin hood in the photograph, making the entire cover weaker. In the next iteration of the jacket, the silhouetted model's face was set against a white background. (This version was also printed on clear acetate.) This muted the lizard

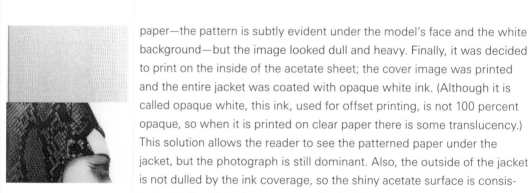

paper—the pattern is subtly evident under the model's face and the white background—but the image looked dull and heavy. Finally, it was decided to print on the inside of the acetate sheet; the cover image was printed and the entire jacket was coated with opaque white ink. (Although it is called opaque white, this ink, used for offset printing, is not 100 percent opaque, so when it is printed on clear paper there is some translucency.) This solution allows the reader to see the patterned paper under the jacket, but the photograph is still dominant. Also, the outside of the jacket is not dulled by the ink coverage, so the shiny acetate surface is consistent with the high-gloss paper on the inside pages.

GODDESS
THE CLASSICAL MODE

THE METROPOLITAN MUSEUM OF ART

The influence of Greco-Roman dress on the history of fashion is the theme of this exhibition catalogue published by the Costume Institute of the Metropolitan Museum of Art. The chiton and the peplos, simple draped garments worn in ancient Greece, were the basis for much of the clothing depicted. Because these ancient garments and their descendents are loose and flowing, the book required a similarly soft, sensuous feel. Uncoated paper was the first choice. The museum, however, favors coated papers, particularly for catalogues like this one that include not only works on paper but also sculpture, painting, and photography, which could look muddy and lose detail. Nevertheless, a few representative artworks were chosen for test prints, and even the paintings looked lush on the uncoated, creamy paper.

All the dresses were photographed the same way: on white mannequins posed against a seamless white background. By digitally manipulating the photographs—lightening the mannequins so that they were similar in tone to the background—the dresses became more prominent as the mannequins faded into the white wall behind them.

The designs of Miuccia Prada often subvert the conventional personae of women through irony, exaggeration, or recontexualization. In dealing with the potent transformative possibilities of dress, her interests focus on the iconography of female identity. In this advertising image, Prada, working with photographer Steven Meisel, mediated classicism through the glamorous 1930s style of the Hollywood portrait photographer George Hurrell. In a surprising coincidence, both dress and pose adumbrate the Cocteau drawing from the same period shown on page 97. That the Cocteau drawing and Grès gown are themselves reiterations of classical forms establishes the attenuated lineage of classical styles.

The ability of the simple conjuction of pleating and girdling to invoke the past is more unexpected in John Galliano's wild conflation of Nordic barbarians and 1930s-style Grecian goddesses, shown on the overleaf. Even the most discrete bits of classical dress—vestigial scraps of pleated cloth and irregular bindings of the midriff—can retain their iconographic power. Like Alexander McQueen and Tom Ford, Galliano has often cited the idealized beauty of classicism to achieve an aggressive feminist identity. The models stranded on a beach in this Steven Klein photograph have elements of Grecian style, and like participants in a mythic version of "Survivor," they exude a strong atavistic ferocity. The copy accompanying the photograph is an overwrought mix of references to reality television and allusions to the isles of Calypso and Circe that establishes a connection to the often lurid classicism encountered in Homer's Odyssey. It reads: "There's an orgy of exhibitionism, a voraciousness of voyeurism, Temptation Island. Hell hath no furies like the sinful silicone seductresses on the Fox Network."

Left: Prada, Italian (founded 1913). Dress, silk jersey, fall–winter 2002. Photograph of Amber Valletta by Steven Meisel courtesy of A+C Anthology. Overleaf: Christian Dior Haute Couture, French (founded 1947), by John Galliano, British (born Gibraltar 1960). Six dresses, silk jersey and chiffon, spring–summer 2001. Group of models photographed by Steven Klein courtesy of Vogue

Madeleine Vionnet is arguably the pre-eminent twentieth-century practitioner of the flou, or draped dressmaking. Her great innovations occurred through her investigations of the bias and of the very structure of cloth to contribute to the ultimate fit of a garment. This image by Irving Penn is from a suite of photographs he made after Diana Vreeland's exhibitions of the nineteen-tens, -twenties, and -thirties. Vionnet's handkerchief dress, of which this white crepe is an example, was made in several variations. Here, four double-layered squares have been rotated ninety degrees to form regular diamond shapes. The diamonds are seamed together vertically at center-front, back, and either side, leaving four sets of triangles that fall in perfect swallowtail folds. The top corners of the diamond shapes are paired and seamed to form the shoulder straps, while the opposite bottom corners form the handkerchief-pointed hem. Vionnet's rotation of the squares results in a transformation of the grain—the direction of the warp and weft of the cloth—into "true" bias, fabric at its most elastic.

Madeleine Vionnet, French (1876–1975). Evening dress, oyster-white crepe romaine, 1919–1920. Photograph: Copyright © 1977 by Irving Penn

A group exhibition at the Museum of Modern Art, New York, in 2008 explored the influence of premixed, industrial paint colors on fine art in the twentieth century. Because forty-four artists spanning almost one hundred years of art history were represented, finding a unifying visual device for the catalogue was challenging. The works included painting, sculpture, video, and installation art. The theme of the show, however, did have a parallel in the offset printing process, so that became an organizing principle for the catalogue. The four standard offset printing colors—cyan, magenta, yellow, and black—were used as design elements throughout. Each of the four divider pages was printed a solid process color.

The curator allotted each artist four or six pages, depending on the number of works represented. The first two pages of each artist's section contain a short essay with comparative illustrations followed by full-page plates. To impose consistency, the artist's name, nationality, country of origin, and date of birth appear in magenta at the top. Below is a quotation from the artist set in large cyan type followed by the catalogue entry, printed in standard black. Using this formula, order was achieved in a volume that otherwise would have been a jumble of imagery from the art of Marcel Duchamp to that of Andy Warhol and Damien Hirst.

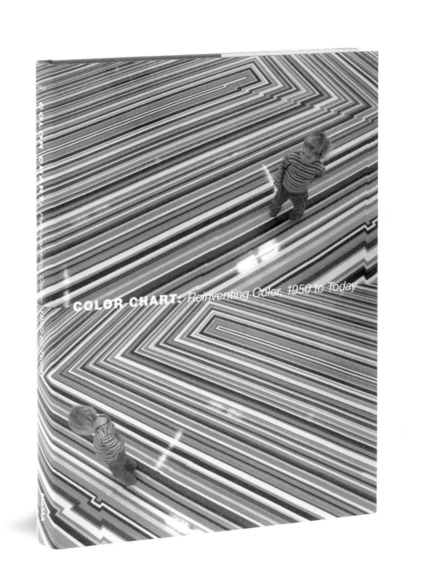

COLOR CHART: *Reinventing Color, 1950 to Today*

Ann Temkin

COLOR CHART: *Reinventing Color, 1950 to Today*

The Museum of Modern Art, New York

Since the tubes of paint used by an artist are manufactured and readymade products we must conclude that all the paintings in the world are readymades aided and also works of assemblage. —Marcel Duchamp, 1961[1]

Fig. 1. Marcel Duchamp and Katherine S. Dreier in the library at her home in West Redding, Connecticut, where Duchamp's *Tu m'* (1918) was reinstalled in 1931. Yale Collection of American Literature, Beinecke Rare Book and Manuscript Library, Yale University

Marcel Duchamp made this now-famous statement at The Museum of Modern Art, concluding his remarks "Apropos of 'Readymades'" at a symposium on the exhibition *The Art of Assemblage*. Duchamp apologized for adding another observation to his "egomaniac's discourse," but he had saved his most provocative comment for last. Whereas "assemblage" was used at the Museum to designate a three-dimensional collage of heterogeneous materials, Duchamp was slyly granting the term a generality that rendered it virtually meaningless. But in so doing he made the important point—so obvious as to be usually ignored—that art is made in an industrial society and not in a vacuum of pure inspiration. It was easy for his listeners to accept that a Joseph Cornell box or a Robert Rauschenberg Combine was made of things, but Duchamp wanted them also to recognize that paint itself was a thing, one that came to a mid-twentieth-century studio from the marketplace.

Duchamp's own acknowledgment of this fact can be traced back in his work to *Tu m'*, of 1918 (plate 1), the last painting he would make. A $1,000 seduction—a commission from the artist and collector Katherine Dreier—brought into the world another painting from the artist who had forsworn the medium four years earlier. Dreier wanted a painting to go above the bookshelf in the library of her Central Park West apartment, and as in a Renaissance commission, the location dictated the work's long, horizontal format (see fig. 1). In this painting, which took about six months to complete, Duchamp provided an overview of his works and concerns of the past several years. He was bringing an end to a chapter in his life; after three years in New York, disliking the wartime climate, he was soon to leave the United States for the neutral country of Argentina. Duchamp left open the meaning of the painting's enigmatic title: "You can add whatever verb you want, as long as it begins with a vowel"—so as to be grammatically correct in French.[2] He later professed dislike for *Tu m'*, saying that "summarizing one's works in a painting is not a very attractive form of activity."[3] It would seem, however, that he was constitutionally prone to summary. Twenty years later—during another wartime displacement, this time from Paris back to New York—Duchamp would spend years rather than months re-creating his oeuvre in miniature and producing it as *Box in a Valise* (1935–41; fig. 2), a "portable museum" that itself is a modern masterpiece of assemblage.[4]

Scholarship on *Tu m'* has explored the painting's engagement with Duchamp's prior work as well as his interest in such subjects as illusion, perspective, and optics, all of which figure into this iconographically and formally complex painting. The focus here is simply its allusion to paint as readymade, which is manifested in the echelon of lozenges extending in classical perspective from the upper-left corner

Fig. 2. Marcel Duchamp. *Box in a Valise (From or by Marcel Duchamp or Rrose Sélavy).* 1935–41. Leather valise containing miniature replicas, photographs, and color reproductions of works by Duchamp, and one "original" drawing (*Large Glass,* collotype on celluloid, 7 ½ x 9 ½" [19 x 23.5 cm]), 16 x 15 x 4" (40.7 x 38.1 x 10.2 cm). The Museum of Modern Art, New York. James Thrall Soby Fund

Fig. 3. Marcel Duchamp. *Apolinère Enameled.* 1916–17. Gouache and graphite on painted tin (advertising sign for Sapolin enamel) mounted on cardboard, 9 ⅝ x 13 ⅜" (24.4 x 33.9 cm). Philadelphia Museum of Art. The Louise and Walter Arensberg Collection

of the canvas to the center. Arturo Schwarz, author of Duchamp's catalogue raisonné, asserted that the lozenges had their source in an oil-paint catalogue but did not specify further.[5] They have the distinct feeling of paint swatches, more real-feeling than an abstract design and completely independent of any sort of chromatic theory or pedagogy. The motley sequence does not appear to have any sense of order, although it recedes to shades of gray as it gets farther away. The perspectival setup causes the samples, when viewed from the side of the painting, to appear to project from the canvas.[6] The actual brass bolt that penetrates the center of the yellow lozenge on top accentuates the feel of a paint salesman's stack of samples.

Duchamp was candid about having hired a sign painter to paint (and sign, with the name "A. Klang") the pointing left hand in the center of the canvas—a pointed objection to the necessity of the artist's hand. He did not mention that he also had delegated the task of painting the lozenges to Yvonne Chastel, his girlfriend at the time, a detail gathered from Duchamp's friend and studio visitor Henri-Pierre Roché.[7] An artist herself, Chastel was a useful surrogate in a painting task that was probably unappealing to Duchamp at that point. Chastel's work on *Tu m'* is curiously prefigured in the assisted readymade *Apolinère Enameled* (1916–17; fig. 3), in an image of a little girl painting her bedstead. *Apolinère Enameled* was made directly on an advertisement for Sapolin enamel, a paint intended for tasks such as refinishing furniture. The use of a girl in the Sapolin placard was typical of paint advertising campaigns that targeted the gentler sex, which proved receptive to the lure of do-it-yourself home improvement.

Tu m' and *Apolinère Enameled* bring together a cast of characters—Marcel Duchamp, A. Klang, Yvonne Chastel, the Sapolin girl—who engage us in the question of what painting is and who does it. Paint and readymade, paint as readymade, painters and artists, painters as artists—all were prescient considerations in Duchamp's work of the mid-1910s and became central artistic preoccupations only three decades later. —A.T.

10. Andy Warhol
Do It Yourself (Flowers). 1962
Acrylic, pencil, and Letraset on linen
69 x 59" (175.3 x 149.9 cm)
Daros Collection, Switzerland

11. Andy Warhol
Do It Yourself (Landscape). 1962
Acrylic, pencil, and Letraset on linen
69 ¾ x 54 ⅛" (177.2 x 137.5 cm)
Museum Ludwig Cologne. Donation Ludwig

Ellsworth Kelly, *Red Curve (Radius 28 inches)*, 1997. Collage on paper, 11 ½ x 12 inches (29.2 x 30.5 cm)

There were multiple challenges in designing this catalogue for the 1996 exhibition "Ellsworth Kelly" at the Solomon R. Guggenheim Museum, New York. First, Kelly's oeuvre ranges from small works on paper to very large paintings and sculptures. The varying proportions of his multiple-panel paintings and shaped canvases made it difficult to determine a trim size and proportions for the book that would best accommodate all the artwork. It was decided that it should be 11 ½ by 10 ¾ inches—slightly wider than a square. This size and shape allowed for most of the works to be reproduced at an appropriately large size. One problem with these dimensions, however, was finding a cover image. Almost every piece in the catalogue was tried, but nothing conformed exactly to the proportions of the jacket. Kelly's reductive forms are an essential aspect of his art, and cropping them fundamentally alters how they are perceived. After the problem was described to him, Kelly created a special image for the jacket, *Red Curve* (*Radius 28 inches*).

While many of Kelly's works are paintings on canvas or wood, he distinguishes between those that are two versus three dimensions. The three-dimensional paintings are often made on canvases with one or more curved sides or different sized canvases joined together. Then there are the many sculptures, which can be mounted on the wall or placed on the floor. It was important that these three categories were made clear to the reader, so each type of work was treated a different way. All the two-dimensional paintings were silhouetted and placed against a white

ELLSWORTH KELLY

GUGGENHEIM MUSEUM

Diane Waldman

Painting and Sculpture

background. The three-dimensional paintings were also silhouetted, but a drop shadow was placed around the art to indicate that it has depth in addition to height and width. Each three-dimensional painting was also shown hanging on a neutral grayish white wall to enhance the illusion of depth. Finally, all the sculptures were shown with both a wall and a floor—even if the sculpture was wall mounted—to distinguish them from the two types of paintings. Treating all the art in one of these three manners also eliminated the problem of dealing with the various environments in which the artworks were photographed. Since Kelly's oeuvre spans more than forty years, the photographs were taken in various locations and had many different kinds of backgrounds. Removing the backgrounds for all the photographs (except the sculptures) created consistency in the presentation of the artist's work.

Ellsworth Kelly: Red Green Blue, Paintings and Studies, 1958–1965, Museum of Contemporary Art San Diego, 2003

The work of the Pop artist Roy Lichtenstein, with its palette of bold primary colors, heavy black outlines, and graphic quality, lends itself to reproduction at a large scale. In this catalogue for a 1993 exhibition at the Guggenheim Museum in New York, the curator wanted not only large reproductions of the paintings and sculptures but also generously sized comparative illustrations. The book's trim size is twelve by twelve inches. Lichtenstein's relationship to other fine artists and comic-book artists is discussed extensively in the text. To invite comparison between the reference materials—works by other artists along with Lichtenstein's own source material—and his artwork, the catalogue is organized into chapters containing text, figures, and plates instead of divided into an essay section and a plate section. To distinguish plates from figures, a rule was devised: all works by Lichtenstein were reproduced as a full page, and reference works were sized to fit one column width.

A major consideration in reproducing his artwork was the variable quality of the original transparencies. Since different photographers had shot them over the course of Lichtenstein's career, the color varied widely in spite of his limited palette. The artist had saved a color palette from early in his career, which was sent to the color separator to be scanned. That scan was used as a guide instead of the transparencies to match the color reproductions, which resulted in more consistent color than otherwise would have been possible.

Mickey Mouse toy from Felix Gonzalez-Torres's collection

Felix Gonzalez-Torres's artwork is defined by its intimacy and poetic character. His oeuvre ranges from small jigsaw puzzles printed with photographs of personal significance to installations consisting of piles of individually wrapped candies or strands of light bulbs. Although the materials he uses are disparate, all his works share a personal quality. The size and proportion of the catalogue that accompanied a 1995 solo exhibition at the Guggenheim Museum in New York are meant to evoke a diary. Rather than separating the catalogue into essay and plate sections, the plates were interspersed throughout the text. This arrangement, along with the catalogue's portable size, was designed to make the experience more like reading a novel than a traditional exhibition catalogue. While some of the artist's works are large installations, all the reproductions are small—there are no full- or two-page spreads—to reinforce the intimacy of the art. Bembo, classic serif typeface, was chosen for the type because of its legibility and the traditional beauty of its letterforms. The cover was wrapped in dark blue silk, and a small reproduction of one of his photographs was tipped-in on the center of the front. A simple vellum jacket, printed with only the title and the museum's name, was wrapped around the book.

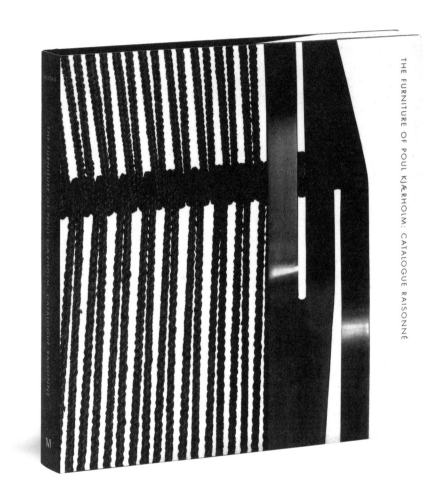

THE FURNITURE OF POUL KJÆRHOLM: CATALOGUE RAISONNÉ

This catalogue raisonné of the work of the Danish furniture designer Poul Kjærholm includes his student projects from the 1950s through the table prototype he designed shortly before his death in 1980. Kjærholm's furniture is spare, elegant, and geometric—qualities reflected in the design of the book. Many of his pieces are based on the square, so a square format was used that complemented most of the furniture.

Poul Kjærholm, "Element" chair, 1951

Kjærholm was a close friend and collaborator of the Danish photographer Keld Helmer-Petersen. The two often installed furniture exhibitions together in Copenhagen, and Helmer-Petersen photographed the majority of Kjærholm's pieces. His period photographs comprise most of the images in the volume. The photographs show the furniture in contemporary settings, as Kjaerholm envisioned it, and give the book visual consistency. Along with the documentary images, some of Helmer-Petersen's fine-art photographs were printed on the end leaves and the divider pages.

Most of the photographs are in black and white, so everything was reproduced using a duotone printing process, which reinforces the mid-century feel of the book, as does the font—Futura, a classic Bauhaus typeface, designed in the 1920s by Paul Renner and popular in the 1950s and 1960s. Its geometric characteristics complement Kjærholm's furniture.

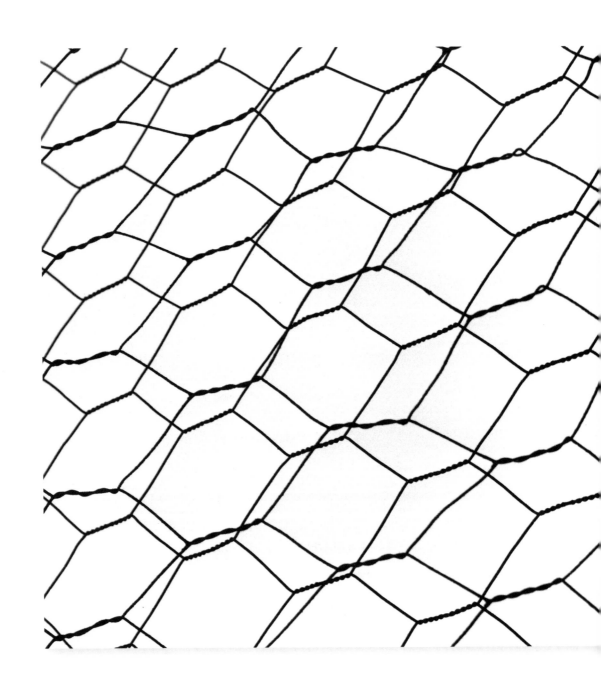

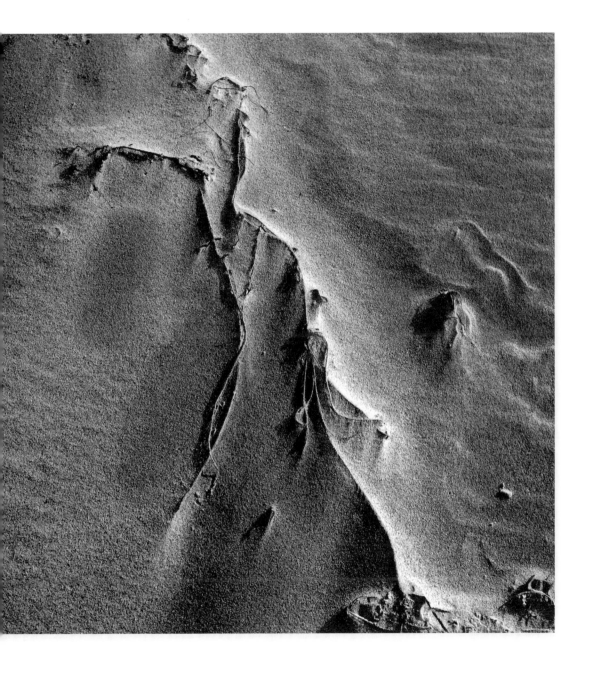

Kjærholm being interviewed, 1954. Left: Unpainted sample, 1953

A view of the trial production at the spring exhibition of the Danish Association of Arts and Crafts, 1954

Molded Aluminum Chair. 1953

Original Dimensions (H x W x D x SH)

63 x 63 x 67 x 37.5 cm (24 ¾ x 24 ¾ x 26 ⅜ x 14 ¾ inches)

Original Materials

Steel tube legs and injection-molded aluminum

Production Dates

1953   Chris Sørensen

2007   R Gallery/Sean Kelly Gallery

Following their collaboration on the upholstered aluminum chair, Kjærholm established a partnership with Chris Sørensen to produce new types of furniture. He immediately began work on a stacking, one-legged chair with a laminated wood seat and a split stem of spring steel, as well as a logo and stationery for their business. The one-legged chair proved to be impractical and never progressed beyond a drawing and a set of small models. Instead, Kjærholm developed a three-legged chair with a molded aluminum shell that combined the aluminum's structural capacity with an ingenious method of production.

Kjærholm's intention was to use an inexpensive material, aluminum, and a simple manufacturing process, molding, to allow economical and large-scale production. This was the first in a series of three chairs in which Kjærholm molded amorphous materials—aluminum, steel wire, and reinforced concrete—into continuous forms combining seat and back in a single shell. In later pieces, he applied this reduction of form to the entire structure, and reached the zenith of his work with organic form. His diversion from assembled frames to molded shells was brief, but the consequences were profound. All three molded chairs provided Kjærholm with lessons in structural forces that were valuable to his later work. He elaborated on the basic model of a molded shell on three steel legs with the design of PK 9, one of his greatest achievements.

The aluminum chair's seat and back were integrated in a thin shell reinforced with a continuous flange along the edge. The flange was deepest at the transition between seat and back, the point of maximum bending stress, and tapered to a narrow lip at the top and bottom. The mold for the shell was made in two parts, with three holes for injecting the metal and allowing the displaced

The artist Alex Katz usually works on a large scale, but most of the pictures at the 2001 exhibition at the Addison Gallery of American Art in Andover, Massachussetts, were small preparatory studies, some only eight by twelve inches. The catalogue reflected the intimate nature of the exhibition. When designing such a catalogue, the size of the reproductions is one of the first things that must be determined. Often, reproductions have to be scaled down, owing to the actual size of the artwork. In this instance, all the paintings were reproduced one-to-one, which meant that many of the images were cropped—an unusual choice, as plates in an exhibition catalogue usually present the full, uncropped image even if details are also provided. (The opposite page illustrates the relationship of the page layouts to the paintings reproduced. The dotted black line is the trim of the catalogue.) The one-to-one reproductions are dramatic and reveal the texture and surface of the brushstrokes. Because some paintings were larger than the nine-by-twelve-inch trim size and had to be cropped, the catalogue contains many full-bleed images. Captions are short, containing only the title and the date of the picture. The text includes a thumbnail checklist of all the works in order to provide both full images and complete caption information.

Green Park, 1954, 8 ⅞ x 12 inches

Ada in Pillbox Hat, 1961, 14 x 19 inches

Green Cap, 1984, 12 ³⁄₁₆ x 17 ¹³⁄₁₆ inches

Ann, 1987, 12 x 9 inches

Peter B., 1988, 11 ⅞ x 14 ³⁄₁₆ inches

Forest, 1991, 12 x 25 inches

Dawn, 1995, 12 x 9 inches

West I, 1998, 10 x 20 inches

In 2006 the sculptor Anish Kapoor received a commission from the Deutsche Guggenheim, Berlin, which resulted in *Memory*, a twenty-four-ton Cor-Ten steel sculpture. Exhibited in Berlin in 2008 and at the Solomon R. Guggenhein Museum, New York, in 2009–10, it was conceived to fit the space at the German venue, where viewers could access it from only three places. It was impossible to walk all the way around the work and experience it in its totality. One of the vantage points was a window cut out of an area in the sculpture that offered a view of its unlit interior.

The exhibition catalogue is in the same proportions as the long, narrow exhibition gallery in Berlin, so the trim size is unusual—seven by twelve inches. It seemed contrary to Kapoor's intention to try to depict *Memory* in a conventional way on the cover since the sculpture is somewhat mysterious. (When the catalogue was being designed there were no photographs of the work, as it was still being made. The catalogues were printed but left unbound while the finished sculpture was photographed. The photos of the installation were printed in a separate signature and then the books were bound.) The solution was to symbolize the viewer's experience of *Memory*. A piece of the rusty-orange steel was scanned and printed on paper that was wrapped around the cover and a square was then die-cut into the front. Black board was used for the cover and the end leaves are black, so the die-cut hole is surrounded by black when the book is closed, alluding to the viewer's experience of looking at the work from the hole cut into its side.

Computer-generated images of the final form of *Memory* (top); sculpture at the Solomon R. Guggenheim Museum, New York (bottom)

This 504-page catalogue for the Solomon R. Guggenheim Museum in New York accompanied a 1999 retrospective of the work of the painter Francesco Clemente, who creates expressionistic, almost dreamlike images using a rich and varied palette. The curator organized the show thematically rather than chronologically. The catalogue is untraditional in that the contributors included not only curators but also a poet, a novelist, and an architect, resulting in a text that is not strictly an art-historical analysis of the artist's oeuvre. The various types of texts required different typesetting treatments.

Clemente's art is heavily influenced by the culture of India; accordingly, the end leaves are bright orange and the divider pages are solid saffron yellow. For a special edition of the catalogue, Clemente drew two sketches of flowers that were used for the front and back covers. The flowers were embroidered in orange and yellow silk on Indian cotton that had been dyed magenta and the cloth was used to wrap the cover.

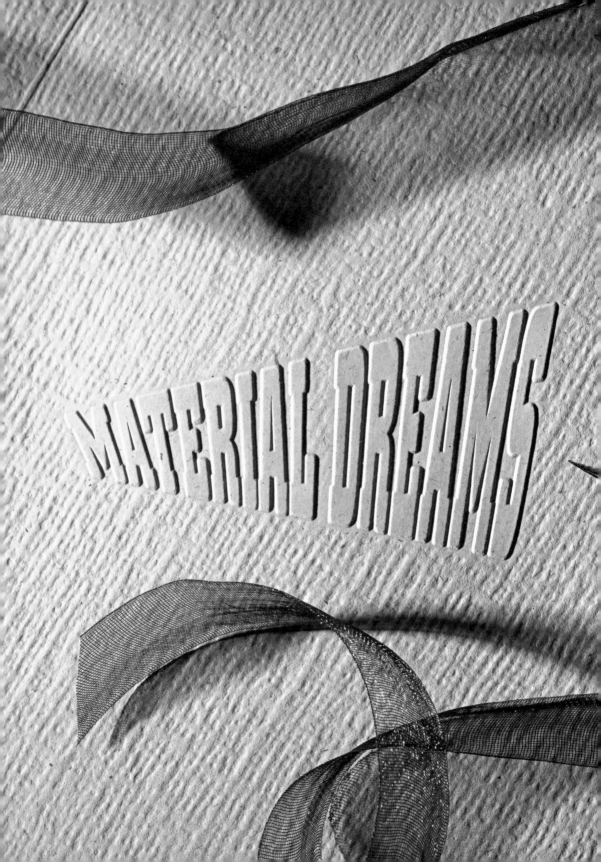

Each of the five artists who participated in "Material Dreams," a 1995 group exhibition at the Gallery at Takashimaya in New York, was commissioned to create an artwork that incorporated textiles. They were still in the midst of creating their pieces when the catalogue was designed, so there were no photographs of the finished works for the plate section. Instead, the artists were given the trim size of the catalogue and asked to send sketches of their works in progress to represent the final pieces. One artist was creating a delicate curtain out of deconstructed silk flowers. To represent it, one silk flower petal was hand-inserted in the bound volume between the pages where a photograph would have been printed. The loose petal necessitated some kind of closure for the book. Two slits were cut on the back cover and a black gossamer ribbon was threaded through the slits and tied in the front.

The text pages were printed on colored vellum to impart a floating, dreamy feel. Each vellum sheet was printed on only one side and then folded in half to reduce the show-through on the text pages and add bulk to the slim seventy-two-page volume. The binding, however, was problematic because vellum does not hold glue well. To avoid the risk of the pages separating from the cover, grommets were used to bind. The asymmetrically placed grommets became a design element and also were in keeping with the textile-themed exhibition.

Jim Hodges, *You*, 1997 (detail). Silk flowers and thread, 216 x 192 inches (548.64 x 187.68 cm)

Screened letter N

This forty-eight-page catalogue for a 1994 group exhibition at the Gallery at Takashimaya has a recycled chipboard cover, which is soft and provides subtle color and texture. It was, however, difficult to print a cover image on this material, so it was not possible to use an artwork from the exhibition. Instead, the exhibition title was to be engraved in large type—sixty points—on the front cover, but, owing to the type size, the engraver was concerned that the ink would peel off if large areas of solid ink were applied. To ensure that the ink would adhere properly to the chipboard, the type for the engraving plate had to be made as a screen rather than a solid, flat area. The screen created tiny voids so that the entire letterform did not fill with ink. These blank areas created enough texture for the ink to adhere to the paper without curling or peeling.

The artwork inside is visually disparate, so design elements were used to unify the catalogue. The design grid, a tool for laying out pages that is usually hidden from the reader, was printed in bright yellow throughout the book. The inside margin is usually left blank, but here it was used as a space for the page numbers and a running footer to indicate the chapter name.

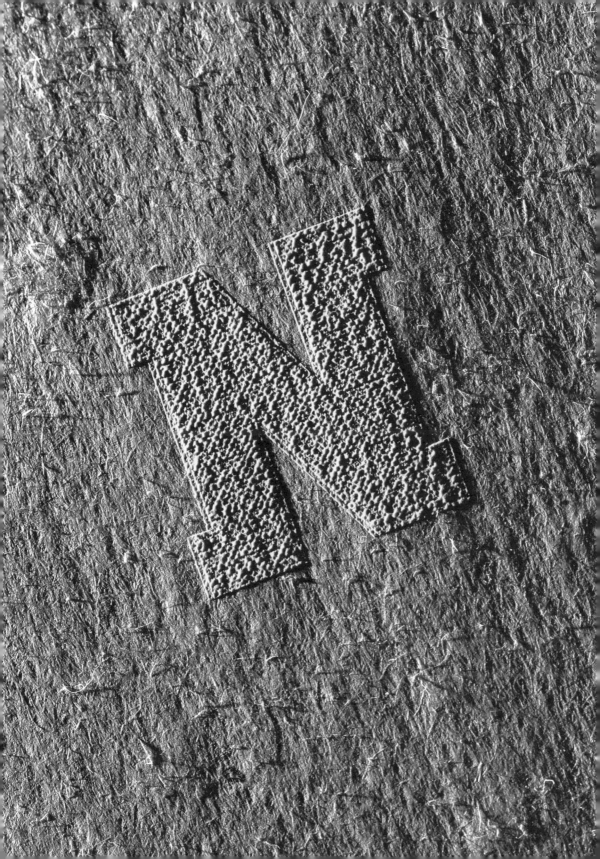

Art in America

July 1985 $4.75

New German Museums / Gohlke's Tulsa Airport Murals / Women Surrealists
Whitney Biennial / Regionalism: Houston vs. Chicago

Art in America

Founded in 1913, the magazine of contemporary art news and criticism *Art in America* was purchased in 1987 by Brant Publications. The masthead in use at the time employed the typeface Trooper Roman, designed by Dave Trooper in the early 1970s, and looked dated, so the new owner wanted it redesigned. After reviewing mastheads from throughout the magazine's long history, a version from the 1960s was chosen as the inspiration for the new design. That masthead, based on the Didot family of typefaces, developed in late eighteenth-century Paris, was elegant and dramatic. The *x* height—the distance between the baseline and the top of the main body of a lowercase letter, usually based on the *x*—was the same height as the horizontal stroke of the capital *A*, making the capital *A*'s the focal point of the type. Torino was used as a starting point for the new masthead. Designed in 1918 by Alessandro Butti, Torino is a display typeface characterized by contrasting very thick and very narrow strokes. Used unaltered, it is a dramatic typeface meant for large signage. In the new design, the difference between the thick and the narrow strokes was made less severe, and the relationship of the capital letters to the lowercase letters was more balanced, so the overall effect is less extreme. In the new version, the *x* height of the lowercase letters is greater than in the old masthead, so the peaks of the capital *A*'s are not as pronounced. As it was designed before digital typesetting was available, the type for the masthead was hand-drawn with brush and ink.

Art in America covers from 1959, 1961, and 1982. Collection of Raphael Rubinstein

Poster design presents an opportunity to explore typography in ways that other print projects—brochures, signage, stationery, catalogues—often do not. The information presented on posters is necessarily edited for brevity, and visual impact is a primary concern. In the posters that follow, typography is the primary design element. It can be used to evoke a previous era in art and design history or to add a human dimension to an otherwise mundane announcement. It may explore the symmetry or balance of letterforms or be a purely decorative element. Alternatively, it can be a compositional focal point around which all the elements of the poster are organized. Color is also an important element in poster design. Often, fewer colors can have a greater impact than a multitude of colors. Sometimes only two strong colors are necessary to create a dramatic visual statement.

NEO-DADA:
REDEFINING
ART '1958-62'

JANUARY 27-MARCH 18, 1995

THE EQUITABLE GALLERY

NEW YORK CITY

SUSAN HAPGOOD, GUEST CURATOR

THIS EXHIBITION IS ORGANIZED BY THE AMERICAN FEDERATION OF ARTS. IT IS A PROJECT OF ART ACCESS, A PROGRAM OF THE AFA WITH MAJOR SUPPORT FROM THE LILA WALLACE-READER'S DIGEST FUND. ADDITIONAL SUPPORT HAS BEEN PROVIDED BY THE NATIONAL PATRONS OF THE AFA. THE EQUITABLE GALLERY IS SPONSORED BY THE EQUITABLE LIFE ASSURANCE SOCIETY OF THE U.S.

We are pleased to announce the consolidation of JCH Graphics with ArtintypeMetro and the opening of our new office. **JCH Group Ltd.**, 352 Park Avenue South, New York, New York 10010. © 212.532.4000 Service 212.532.4718 FAX 212.689.8568

Coming of Age:

Selections from The Scholastic
Art & Writing Awards of 1995
March 15 - April 20, 1996

The Equitable Gallery
787 Seventh Avenue at 52nd Street
New York City

These investigations into the square arose from experimenting with a strict rule for implementation to derive an array of patterns. The basic rule was simple: take one square and quarter it to create four smaller squares of equal size. The smaller square was also quartered, creating four more squares that were one-sixteenth the size of the original square. Then that square was also quartered to create four more squares, which were a sixty-fourth of the size of the original square. One of each of the smaller squares was placed within the larger square to create the basic unit. Each unit could also be reduced by 50 percent, 25 percent, or 12.5 percent to create smaller building blocks for the overall pattern. Rotating the units 90, 180, or 270 degrees also resulted in variations in the pattern. After the rule for replicating the shapes was implemented, each square was given a unique solid color or a graphic image. These colorful elements created a new pattern in addition to the square.

For an exhibition at the University of Akron, the same idea was translated into three dimensions. A cube was used instead of a square, but the same rules applied. The largest cube was twelve by twelve by twelve inches, which, when cut, yielded six-inch-square cubes. Some of the six-inch cubes were then cut into three-inch-square cubes. These three sizes were then used to create different patterns, incorporating the added dimension of height. Each group of cubes sat on top of a square area of black sand placed on a carpet of Astroturf, creating a synthetic garden for viewers to walk through.

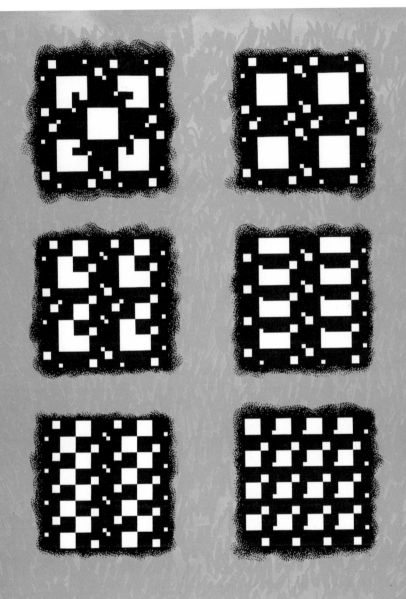

S QUARE

TAKAAKI
MATSUMOTO

INSTALLATION
10/31-11/17, 1988

THE UNIVERSITY
OF AKRON

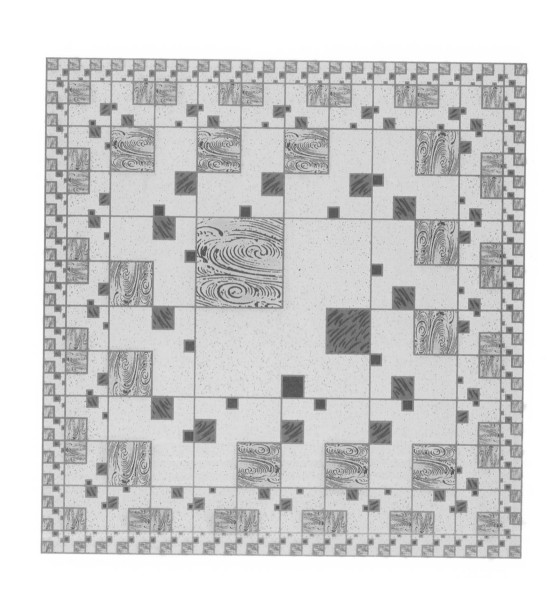

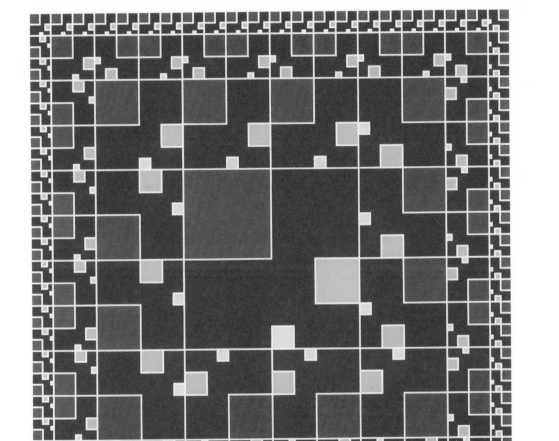

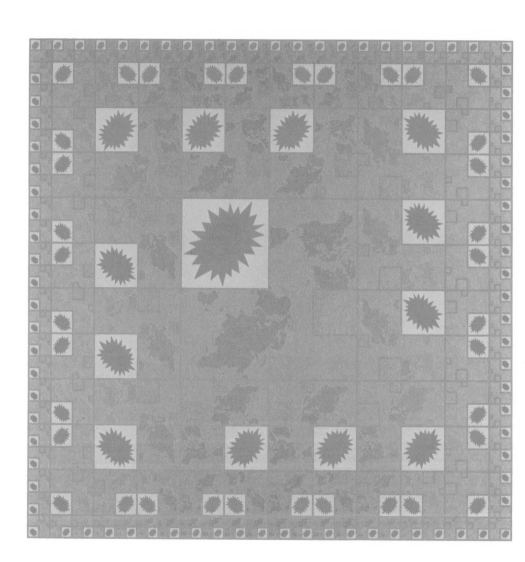

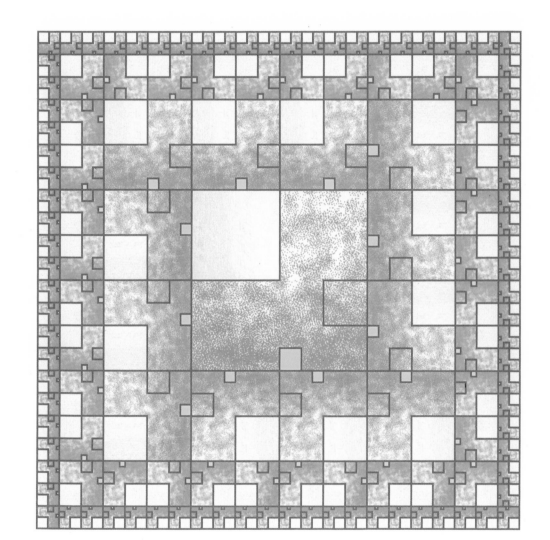

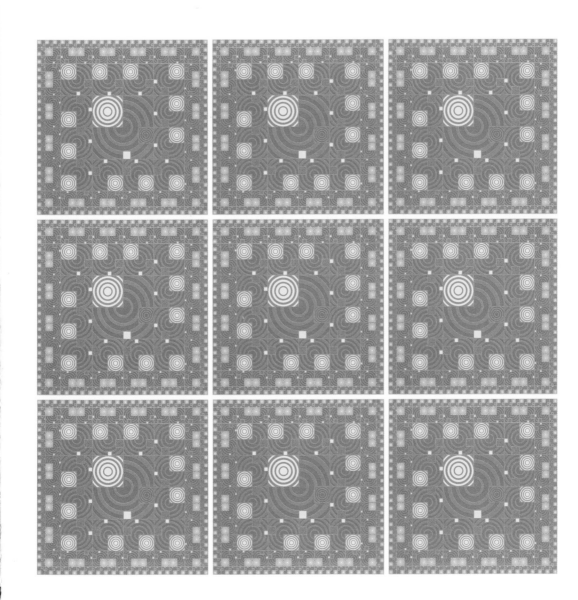

(pp. 16–21)
Boundless, 2005–6
Client: Art Center College of Design,
 Pasadena, Calif.
Pages: 128
Paper: (cover) Navajo Brilliant White;
 (text) Finch Opaque Vellum
Size: 6 x 9 inches (15.2 x 22.8 cm)
Printing: (cover) two-color offset and
 die-cutting; (text) two-color offset
Typeface: Univers
Printed in the United States

(pp. 22–23)
Art Center College of Design
 recruitment catalogue, 2007–8
Client: Art Center College of Design,
 Pasadena, Calif.
Pages: 226
Paper: (cover) F1 Card; (coated text
 pages) Raicho Dull Art; (uncoated
 text pages) Color W/F Ivory;
 (shipping carton) custom envelope
 fabricated from clear bubble wrap
Size: 10 ¼ x 8 ½ inches (25.8 x 21.5 cm)
Printing: (cover) two-color offset and
 die-cutting; (text) four-color process
Typeface: Univers
Printed in Japan

(pp. 24–31)
Art Center College of Design
 recruitment catalogue, 2009–10
Client: Art Center College of Design,
 Pasadena, Calif.
Pages: 152
Paper: Finch Opaque Smooth Bright
 White
Size: 10 ¼ x 14 ¼ inches (25.9 x 36.2 cm)
Typefaces: Univers
Printed in the United States

(pp. 32–33)
Dot Magazine, 2005–8
Client: Art Center College of Design,
 Pasadena, Calif.
Pages: 32
Paper: (cover) Finch Fine Ultra Smooth
 Bright White; (text) Finch Opaque
 Vellum Bright White
Size: 8 x 10 inches (20.3 x 25.4 cm)
Typefaces: various
Printed in the United States

(pp. 38–39)
Identity and stationery system, 1993
Client: Maharam
Paper: Crane's Crest Fluorescent
 White Wove
Printing: three-color engraving
Typeface: Futura
Printed in the United States

(p. 56)
Identity and stationery system, 1993
Client: Merrill C. Berman Collection
Paper: Crane's Crest Natural White
 Wove
Printing: two-color letterpress
Typeface: Futura
Printed in the United States

(p. 57)
Identity and stationery system, 1996
Client: DimsonHomma
Paper: Crane's Crest Fluorescent
 White Wove
Printing: two-color engraving and
 die-cutting
Typefaces: hand-drawn custom type
 (logo), Garamond
Printed in the United States

(p. 58)
Identity and stationery system, 1998
Client: Bendheim
Paper: Crane's Crest Fluorescent
 White Wove
Printing: one-color metallic-ink
 engraving
Typeface: hand-drawn custom type
Printed in the United States

(p. 59)
Identity and stationery system, 1991
Client: Pen Plus Inc.
Paper Crane's Crest Fluorescent White
 Wove
Printing: one-color engraving and
 embossing
Typeface: Helvetica
Printed in the United States

(p. 60)
Identity and stationery system, 1988
Client: I Pezzi Dipinti
Paper: Strathmore Writing Natural
 White
Printing: one-color offset and one-
 color metallic-ink engraving
Typeface: Copperplate
Printed in the United States

(p. 61)
Identity and stationery system, 2001
Client: Sugimoto Studio
Paper: Crane's Crest Fluorescent
 White
Printing: one-color engraving and
 foil-stamping
Typeface: Univers
Printed in the United States

(p. 62)
Invitation, 1983
Client: Knoll International

Paper: Mohawk Superfine Ultrawhite
 Eggshell
Printing: one-color offset and
 die-cutting
Typeface: Bodoni
Printed in the United States

(pp. 62–63)
Holiday card, 1983
Client: Knoll International
Paper: Mohawk Superfine Ultrawhite
 Eggshell
Printing: one-color metallic-ink
 engraving and die-cutting
Typeface: Helvetica
Printed in the United States

(pp. 64–65)
Poster and invitation, 1984
Client: Knoll International
Paper: Mohawk Poseidon
Printing: four-color offset and
 die-cutting
Typeface: Bodoni
Printed in the United States

(p. 65)
Brochure, 1984
Client: Knoll International
Paper: Potlatch Vintage Velvet
Printing: (cover) three-color offset
 and die-cutting; (text) four-color
 offset
Typeface: Helvetica
Printed in the United States

(pp. 76–77)
Identity and stationery system, 1995
Client: Acadia Summer Arts Program
Paper: Strathmore Writing Natural
 White Wove and Ultimate White
 Wove
Printing: four-color letterpress
Typefaces: hand-drawn type (logo),
 Futura
Printed in the United States

(pp. 78–79)
Identity and stationery system, 2003
Client: Fabric Workshop and
 Museum
Paper: Strathmore Writing Ultimate
 White Wove
Printing: three-color offset and laser
 die-cutting
Typeface: Franklin Gothic
Printed in the United States

(pp. 82–87)
*New Material as New Media: The
 Fabric Workshop and Museum*, 2002
Publisher: Fabric Workshop and
 Museum, Philadelphia

*Unless otherwise noted, all printing
is four-color offset.*

Pages: 320
Paper and materials: (cover) Deluxe
    Satin bookbinding cloth; (paper)
    Kinfuji Satin; (case) custom designed
    brushed aluminum with die-cut
    holes and piano hinge
Size: 10¾ x 13 inches (27.3 x 33 cm)
Typeface: Franklin Gothic
Printed in Japan

(pp. 88–95)
Ed Ruscha: Industrial Strength, 2008
Publisher: Fabric Workshop and
    Museum, Philadelphia
Pages: 60
Paper: A-Plan Natural White
Size: 11¾ x 10 inches (29.8 x 25.5 cm)
Typeface: Minion
Printed in Japan

(pp. 96–97)
Time Exposed, 1991
Publisher: Kyoto Shoin, Kyoto
Pages: 54
Paper: (photographs) Mitsubishi Real
    Art Both Side; (mounting paper)
    Peach Kent
Printing and fabrication:
    (photographs) four-color offset;
    (mounting paper) blind embossing;
    (case) custom designed brushed
    aluminum with piano hinge
Size: 18¼ x 13⅞ inches (46.4 x 35.2 cm)
Typeface: Garamond
Folios printed in Japan; case
    fabricated in the United States

(pp. 98–103)
Theaters: Hiroshi Sugimoto, 2000
Publisher: Sonnabend Gallery, New
    York; and Eyestorm.com, London
Pages: 224
Paper: Mohawk Superfine Eggshell
Printing and fabrication: (cover) Day-
    Glo ink silk-screen and foil stamping;
    (text) four-color dry-trap offset;
    (case) custom-designed brushed
    aluminum
Size: 10⅞ x 12 inches (27.7 x 30.3 cm)
Typeface: Univers
Printed in the United States

(pp. 104–5)
Sea of Buddha by Hiroshi Sugimoto,
    1997
Publisher: Sonnabend Gallery,
    Sonnabend Sundell Editions, New
    York
Pages: 120
Paper and materials: (cover) brushed
    aluminum; (text) Van Nouveau
Printing: (cover) one-color silk-screen;
    (text) three-color offset

Size: 6 x 9⅜ inches (15.3 x 23.9 cm)
Typeface: Garamond
Printed in Japan

(pp. 106–7)
Sugimoto: Architecture, 2005
Publisher: Museum of Contemporary
    Art, Chicago
Pages: 168
Paper: (cover) Yupo Translucent Text;
    (text) Phoenix Motion Xantur
Size: 10⅞ x 12 inches (27.6 x 30.5 cm)
Typeface: Univers
Printed in Germany

(pp. 108–13)
Hiroshi Sugimoto, 1997
Publisher: Hatje Cantz, Germany
Pages: 368
Paper and materials: (jacket and text)
    Scheufelen Phoenix Motion Xantur;
    (cloth for trade edition cover)
    Setalux; (cloth for special edition)
    silk twill; (case) brushed aluminum
Size: 9⅞ x 11 inches (25.1 x 27.9 cm)
Typeface: Univers
Printed in Germany

(pp. 114–17)
Joe, 2006
Pubisher: Pulitzer Foundation for the
    Art, Saint Louis
Pages: 88
Paper: Scheufelen Phoenix Motion
    Xantur
Size: 11½ x 14½ inches (29.2 x 36.8 cm)
Typeface: Bembo
Printed in Italy

(pp. 118–21)
Wild: Fashion Untamed, 2004
Publisher: Metropolitan Museum of
    Art, New York
Pages: 180
Paper: (jacket) Pet Film; (cover)
    Skivertex Pellaq Iguana Royal
    Oyster; (text) Kyesung Tri-Pine
    Deluxe Gloss
Size: 6¾ x 9⅞ inches (17.1 x 25.1 cm)
Typeface: Univers
Printed in Japan

(pp. 122–27)
Goddess: The Classical Mode, 2003
Publisher: Metropolitan Museum of
    Art, New York
Pages: 224
Paper: Mohawk Superfine White
    Eggshell
Size: 9 x 11¾ inches (22.9 x 29.8 cm)
Typeface: Goudy Old Style
Printed in Spain

(pp. 128–35)
*Color Chart: Reinventing Color, 1950 to
    Today,* 2008
Publisher: Museum of Modern Art,
    New York
Pages: 248
Paper: Gold East Matte
Size: 9 x 12 inches (22.9 x 30.5 cm)
Typefaces: Helvetica, Janson
Printed in Singapore

(pp. 136–39)
Ellsworth Kelly, 1997
Publisher: Solomon R. Guggenheim
    Museum, New York
Pages: 336
Paper: DC Satin
Size: 11½ x 10¾ inches (29.2 x 27.3 cm)
Typefaces: Univers, Sabon
Printed in Germany

(pp. 140–43)
Roy Lichtenstein, 1993
Publisher: Solomon R. Guggenheim
    Museum, New York
Pages: 394
Paper: CD Satin
Size: 11⅝ x 11¾ inches (29.5 x 29.8 cm)
Typefaces: Bembo, Meta
Printed in Germany

(pp. 144–45)
Felix Gonzalez-Torres, 1995
Publisher: Solomon R. Guggenheim
    Museum, New York
Pages: 234
Paper: Scheufelen BVS Matt White
Size: 6 x 9 inches (15.2 x 22.9 cm)
Typeface: Bembo
Printed in Germany

(pp. 146–51)
*The Furniture of Poul Kjærholm:
    Catalogue Raisonné,* 2007
Publisher: Gregory R. Miller & Co.,
    New York
Pages: 224
Paper: A-Plan Natural White
Size: 8⅝ x 8⅝ inches (21.9 x 21.9 cm)
Typeface: Futura
Printed in Japan

(pp. 152–53)
Alex Katz: Small Paintings, 2001
Publisher: Addison Gallery of
    American Art, Phillips Academy,
    Andover, Mass.
Pages: 88
Paper: Scheufelen Job Paralux White
Size: 9 x 12 inches (22.9 x 30.5 cm)
Typeface: Garamond
Printed in Italy

(pp. 154–55)
Anish Kapoor: Memory, 2008
Publisher: Solomon R. Guggenheim
    Museum, New York
Pages: 128
Paper: M Real Eurobulk Matt
Size: 7 x 12 inches (17.8 x 30.5 cm)
Typeface: Garamond
Printed in Germany

(pp. 156–57)
Francesco Clemente, 1999
Publisher: Solomon R. Guggenheim
    Museum, New York
Pages: 504
Paper and materials: (cover) custom-
    dyed and embroidered Indian
    cotton; (text) Scheufelen Phoenix
    Motion Xantic
Size: 9¾ x 11⅝ inches (24.8 x 29.5 cm)
Typefaces: Helvetica, Janson
Printed in Germany

(pp. 158–59)
Material Dreams, 1995
Publisher: Gallery at Takashimaya,
    New York
Paper: (cover) French Cordtone
    Natural Speckletone; (text) Neenah
    Blue and Neenah Sepia; (plates)
    Neenah Recycled Natural White
Size: 5¾ x 8 inches (14.6 x 20.3 cm)
Typefaces: hand-drawn typeface
    (cover), Janson, Courier
Printed in United States

(pp. 160–61)
Reorientations: Looking East, 1994
Publisher: Gallery at Takashimaya,
    New York
Paper: (cover) French Paper Carton;
    (text) Mohawk Super Fine
Size: 8⅜ x 11⅝ inches (21.3 x 29.5 cm)
Typefaces: Janson, City, Courier,
    Meta
Printed in the United States

Kippy Stroud has been an indefatigable supporter of mine since we met in 1995. I have immensely enjoyed the projects we have worked on together, both for the Fabric Workshop and Museum and A.S.A.P., as well as the friendship that has developed over the years. I am very grateful that she offered to publish this volume on my work.

Harold Koda has been a great friend and collaborator during the thirty years I have known him. I have had the pleasure of designing many publications for the Costume Institute, and Harold's combination of deep intellect and wit always inspires me. I am honored that he wrote the introduction for this volume, which eloquently captures my approach to design.

Many thanks are also owed to Mikio Sekita, a friend since we both attended Art Center College of Design in the 1970s and who took almost all the photographs for the book. His generosity and patience have been invaluable to me.

A decade-long collaboration with Amy Wilkins has played an inestimable role in the office and in my work. She has earned my respect and admiration for her diligent attention to detail, creative thinking, and tireless responsibility for every aspect of a project. In addition to her dedication to managing the business and individual endeavors, she has written this book with intelligent description and insightful detail.

Without the clients, artists, photographers, writers, and editors with whom I have collaborated over the last thirty years, this body of work would not exist. Although the list is far too long to provide here, I am grateful to every one of them.

I am deeply indebted to Michael McGinn, with whom I first started an independent design consultancy. His design sensibility, ethical compass, and meticulous attention to detail have had a great impact on my design and business practices.

The designer Hisami Aoki has capably assisted me in projects big and small for the last five years and endured endless changes, revisions, and overhauls of projects with dedication and good humor.

I would like to thank all the designers and office managers who have worked for me: Delphine Barringer, Jennifer Batty, Carrie Berman, Lisa Candela, Allison Choate, Tina Ginesini, Kathryn Hammill, Nae Hayakawa, Branwen Jones, Watchara Kantamala, Whitney Lowe, Larissa Nowicki, Bernard Ong, Lizelle Ortigas, Keith Price, John Rodrigues, Mikio Sakai, Thanh X. Tran, and Caroline Woolley. Thanks are also owed to the many interns who have volunteered their time over the years.

Finally, the love and support of my wife, Julie, and my children, Maximilian and Julia, have meant everything to me.

Takaaki Matsumoto

In 1987 Takaaki Matsumoto co-founded M Plus M Incorporated, a consulting firm specializing in graphic and product design. In 1994 he became the principal and president of the company, renaming it Matsumoto Incorporated. He resides in New York with his wife and two children.

Takaaki, who was born in Japan, came to the United States in 1974. Prior to establishing M Plus M, he attended the Art Center College of Design in Pasadena, California, and began his professional career as a designer at Gips and Balkind in New York (1980–82). He then served as the art director for Knoll International (1982–87). He has received numerous honors from such prestigious institutions as the American Institute of Graphic Arts, Society of Typographic Arts, Type Directors Club, and Art Directors Club of New York and Los Angeles. In 2003 and 2004 he received the "Franny" prize from the American Association of Museum's Publication Competition.

In 1989 Takaaki was given a one-man show of his work, for which he received a commission for an installation, at the University of Akron, Ohio, and the Fashion Institute of Technology, New York. He was also invited to lecture and show his work at the university as well as at New York's chapter of the American Institute of Graphic Arts, School of Visual Arts, and Fashion Institute of Technology.

Takaaki's work has been featured in various national and international publications, including *Communication Arts, ID Magazine, Graphis, Metropolis, FP Design, Creator's File, Portfolio Design, Graphis Annual, Graphis Posters, STA 100 Show, Tokyo Alpha Polis*, *International Contemporary Designers, Design Journal* (Korea), *Yomiuri Newspaper, Graphic Design: New York, Design Exchange: Hong Kong,* and *The 20th Century Poster—Design of the Avant-Garde* (Abbeville Press).

Takaaki's work is included in the collections of various museums, such as the Library of Congress, Chicago Athenaeum (Museum of Architecture and Design), Montreal Museum of Decorative Arts, Image for Peace (Montreal), Cooper-Hewitt National Design Museum, and Berman Collection.

The Acadia Summer Arts Program—commonly referred to as A.S.A.P., Kippy's Kamp, and Kamp Kippy—is an internationally known summer artists' residency located in breathtaking Acadia National Park, on Mount Desert Island, Maine. Since 1993 the program has furnished invitees with the time, space, and resources to rejuvenate their creative practices. Each year, A.S.A.P. convenes an impressive array of artists and arts professionals, including museum directors, curators, architects, painters, sculptors, filmmakers, musicians, poets, dancers, and historians. The island is dotted with A.S.A.P.'s private cottages, which guests are free to use as either peaceful work space or for simple rest and relaxation. Most of the guests' time is unstructured, but the program provides weekly communal activities—dinners, guest lectures, and boat excursions to the surrounding islands—and annual public events such as exhibitions, film screenings, dance performances, and concerts.

Marion "Kippy" Boulton Stroud, the founder of A.S.A.P., has had a lifelong passion for supporting and facilitating artistic production. In 1977 she founded the Fabric Workshop and Museum in Philadelphia, where she currently serves as artistic director. Having spent summers on Mount Desert Island since childhood, Kippy wanted to share the beautiful Maine landscape with her friends and colleagues. Beginning as a small gathering in Kippy's coastal home, Shore Cottage, the program has blossomed into a summer-long influx of more than three hundred guests each year. Consequently, the physical space has evolved into a complex of studios, offices, and lecture facilities, designed by Robert Venturi, Denise Scott Brown, and the late Steven Izenour of Venturi, Scott Brown and Associates. Despite this growth, the intimate, familial quality of A.S.A.P. remains.